indexed

P I A N O • V O C A L

HOLLYWOOD MUSICALS YEAR·BY·YEAR

VOLUME 1
1927 TO 1939

The essays about each film are excerpted from the book *Hollywood Musicals Year by Year* by author Stanley Green (Hal Leonard Corporation, 1990) with additional text on recent movies by Richard Walters.

This publication is not for sale in the E.C. and/or Australia or New Zealand.

HAL•LEONARD™ CORPORATION

7777 W. BLUEMOUND RD. P.O. BOX 13819 MILWAUKEE, WI 53213

Copyright © 1995 by HAL LEONARD CORPORATION
International Copyright Secured   All Rights Reserved

For all works contained herein:
Unauthorized copying, arranging, adapting, recording or public performance is an infringement of copyright.
Infringers are liable under the law.

ISBN 0-7935-3206-X

Hollywood Musicals Year by Year 1927-1939
Index By Song Title

HOLLYWOOD MUSICALS YEAR BY YEAR 1927-1939
CHRONOLOGICAL INDEX

My Mammy

FROM THE JAZZ SINGER

Words by SAM M. LEWIS and JOE YOUNG
Music by WALTER DONALDSON

© 1920 IRVING BERLIN, INC.
© Renewed 1948 WAROCK CORP., BOURNE CO. and DONALDSON PUBLISHING CO.
All Rights Reserved

The Jazz Singer

Screenplay: Alfred A. Cohen
Titles: Jack Jarmuth
Produced by: Darryl F. Zanuck for Warner Bros.
Directed by: Alan Crosland
Photography: Hal Mohr
Cast: Al Jolson, May McAvoy, Warner Oland, Eugenie
    Besserer, Otto Lederer, Bobby Gordon, Roscoe Karns,
    Cantor Josef Rosenblatt, William Demarest, Myrna Loy
Songs: "Kol Nidre" (trad.); "Dirty Hands, Dirty Face"
    (James Monaco, Edgar Leslie, Grant Clarke); "Toot, Toot,
    Tootsie!" (Ted Fiorito, Robert King-Gus Kahn); "Yahrzeit"
    (trad.); "Blue Skies" (Irving Berlin); "Mother of Mine, I
    Still Have You" (Louis Silvers-Clarke); "My Mammy"
    (Walter Donaldson-Sam Lewis, Joe Young)
Released: October 1927; 89 minutes

Al Jolson belting out "Toot, Toot, Tootsie!" in a San Francisco nightspot.

"Wait a minute! Wait a minute! You ain't heard nothin' yet…" The first words spoken in a feature-length motion picture were uttered by an exuberant Al Jolson in *The Jazz Singer* just before launching into "Toot, Toot, Tootsie!" in a San Francisco nightclub. Thus the film—even though only its musical sequences and a few bits of dialogue were wired for sound—gets the credit as not only the first "talkie" but also the first screen musical. Since music is the one element impossible to convey in silent movies, it was both inevitable and logical that when the screen found its voice it would also burst into song.

The historic premiere of *The Jazz Singer* took place on October 6, 1927, at the Warner Theatre in New York. Its genesis occurred five years earlier as a short story, "The Day of Atonement" by Samson Raphaelson, who had modeled the central character on Al Jolson. The author subsequently adapted the story into a play, first called *Prayboy* then *The Jazz Singer*, with Jolson himself set for the leading role. But a disagreement between star and playwright brought about Jolson's replacement by George Jessel. Opening on Broadway in the fall of 1925, the play enjoyed a run of over 300 performances.

In 1926, Warner Bros., after purchasing the Vitaphone sound-on-disc process from Western Electric, released a silent movie, *Don Juan*, which was the first full-length dramatic film with a background score. The studio had already secured the screen rights to *The Jazz Singer* for $50,000, with Jessel signed to repeat his part, when Sam Warner decided to add audible musical sequences. When Jessel broke his contract because he felt the addition of sound entitled him to more money, the studio turned to Jolson to play Jakie Rabinowitz, the cantor's son, who, much to the distress of his parents, runs away from home to become jazz singer Jack Robin. After his father dies, however, Jakie gives up his big chance to star in a Broadway revue to assume the cantor's duties for the Yom Kippur services.

Though its emphasis on mother love makes it unduly maudlin, the film follows the general design of the stage production, except for a tacked-on ending that shows Jack Robin, some years later, belting out "My Mammy" in blackface to his own beaming mammy in the audience at a Broadway revue. The film's only spoken dialogue occurs earlier when Jackie unexpectedly returns home, sings "Blue Skies" for his mother, and then interrupts the song to tell her of all the wonderful things he is now able to do for her. Even the practice of voice dubbing began with *The Jazz Singer*, since the singing of Warner Oland, as the cantor, actually emanated from the soundtrack voice of Joseph Deskay.

In 1945, Warners planned a remake of *The Jazz Singer*, but shelved it because of Columbia's imminent production of *The Jolson Story*. The studio did release an updated version in 1952, with Danny Thomas in the title role (renamed Jerry Golding), Peggy Lee, and Eduard Franz as the cantor. A third variation, in 1980, co-starred Neil Diamond (now Jess Robin, né Rabinovitch), Laurence Olivier as his improbable procreator, and Lucie Arnaz as the love interest, and reset the story in the milieu of the pop-rock world. In both remakes, not only does the father live but he becomes an enthusiastic booster of his son's career.

Sountrak ST. MGM/UA VC.

1927

THE SINGING FOOL

Music: Ray Henderson, etc.
Lyrics: B. G. DeSylva & Lew Brown, etc.
Screenplay: C. Graham Baker
Titles: Joseph Jackson
Produced by: Darryl F. Zanuck for Warner Bros.
Directed by: Lloyd Bacon
Choreography: Larry Ceballos
Photography: Byron Haskin
Cast: Al Jolson, Betty Bronson, Josephine Dunn, Davey Lee
Songs: "It All Depends on You"; "I'm Sitting on Top of the World"; "There's a Rainbow 'Round My Shoulder" (Dave Dreyer-Billy Rose, Al Jolson); "Golden Gate" (Joseph Meyer-Dreyer-Rose-Jolson); "Sonny Boy" (with Jolson)
Released: September 1928; 101 minutes

Al Jolson and babe.

Though it was still only a part-talkie, *The Singing Fool* became the first sound film to gross $4 million in U.S. and Canadian theatre rentals—and it would not be outgrossed until ten years later when it was overtaken by *Snow White and the Seven Dwarfs*. In this sentimental tale Al Jolson plays a singing waiter who rises in show business, then hits the skids when his wife leaves him. There's further grief when his three-year-old son (Davey Lee) dies, but he bounces back with the aid of a good woman. The movie was the first with sound to show the screen's potential for launching song hits, since it was responsible for introducing "There's a Rainbow 'Round My Shoulder" and "Sonny Boy" (which its creators, DeSylva, Brown and Henderson, had written half-jokingly to see how many mawkish clichés they could pack into one lyric).

1928

Sonny Boy
FROM THE SINGING FOOL

Words and Music by AL JOLSON, B.G. DeSYLVA,
LEW BROWN and RAY HENDERSON

Copyright © 1928 by Chappell & Co., Stephen Ballentine Music Publishing Co. and Ray Henderson Music
Copyright Renewed
International Copyright Secured   All Rights Reserved

Sunny Side Up

Music: Ray Henderson
Lyrics: B.G. DeSylva & Lew Brown
Screenplay: B.G. DeSylva, Lew Brown & Ray Henderson
Produced by: B.G. DeSylva for Fox
Directed by: David Butler
Choreography: Seymour Felix
Photography: Ernest Palmer, John Schmitz (part Multicolor)
Cast: Janet Gaynor, Charles Farrell, El Brendel, Marjorie White, Frank Richardson, Sharon Lynn, Mary Forbes, Jackie Cooper
Songs: "I'm a Dreamer, Aren't We All?"; "Sunny Side Up"; "You Find the Time, I'll Find the Place"; "Turn on the Heat"; "If I Had a Talking Picture of You"
Released: October 1929; 115 minutes

The steady outpouring of musical films in 1929 prompted a steady stream of Hollywood-bound Broadway songwriters. Three early arrivals were B.G. DeSylva, Lew Brown and Ray Henderson who provided both songs and screenplay for *Sunny Side Up* (also written *Sunnyside Up*), which they fashioned along the familiar Cinderella lines that had long provided librettos for stage musicals. In this case, it's poor Molly Carr (Janet Gaynor), from New York's Yorkville, who manages to meet rich playboy Jack Cromwell (Charles Farrell) from Southhampton, and so impresses him with her singing of "Sunny Side Up" ("If you meet with gloom, don't fall down and go boom") that he invites her to appear in a lavish charity show to be presented on his family's estate. In the show, they express their romantic feelings in "If I Had a Talking Picture of You" and Miss Gaynor does a solo turn to the wistful "I'm a Dreamer, Aren't We All?" The movie also offers the first purely cinematic production number in "Turn on the Heat." The scene opens in the frozen North where chorus girls emerge from igloos wearing heavy furs, then disrobe to brief tops and bottoms as the snow melts, grass grows, palm trees sprout, steam rises from the ground, and even a fire breaks out. When last seen, the girls escape the conflagration by diving into a lagoon.

If I Had a Talking Picture of You

FROM SUNNY SIDE UP

Words and Music by RAY HENDERSON,
LEW BROWN and B.G. DeSYLVA

I talk to your pho-to-graph each day.
All I have to keep me com-pa-ny

You should hear the love-ly things I say.
is the pho-to-graph you gave to me.

But I've thought how hap-py I would be
I pro-pose a thou-sand plans, but oh,

Copyright © 1929, by Chappell & Co., Ray Henderson Music Co. and Stephen Ballentine Music Co.
Copyright Renewed
International Copyright Secured   All Rights Reserved

Paramount on Parade

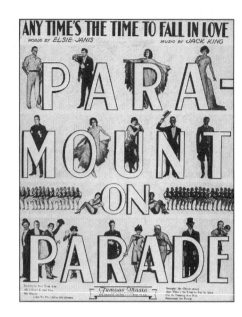

Produced by: Albert S. Kaufman for Paramount

Directed by: Dorothy Arzner, Otto Brower, Edmund Goulding, Victor Heerman, Edwin Knopf, Rowland Lee, Ernst Lubitsch, Lothar Mendes, Victor Schertzinger, A. Edward Sutherland, Frank Tuttle

Choreography: David Bennett, Marion Morgan

Photography: Harry Fischbeck, Victor Milner (part Technicolor)

Cast: Richard Arlen, Jean Arthur, Mischa Auer, George Bancroft, Clara Bow, Evelyn Brent, Mary Brian, Clive Brook, Virginia Bruce, Nancy Carroll, Ruth Chatterton, Maurice Chevalier, Gary Cooper, Leon Errol, Stuart Erwin, Kay Francis, Skeets Gallagher, Mitzi Green, Phillips Holmes, Helen Kane, Dennis King, Abe Lyman Orch., Fredric March, Nino Martini, Mitzi Mayfair, Jack Oakie, Warner Oland, Zelma O'Neal, Eugene Pallette, William Powell, Charles "Buddy" Rogers, Lillian Roth, Fay Wray

Songs: "Any Time's the Time to Fall in Love" (Jack King-Elsie Janis); "My Marine" (Richard Whiting-Ray Egan); "All I Want Is Just One" (Whiting-Robin); "Let's Drink to the Girl of My Dreams" (Abel Baer-L. Wolfe Gilbert); "I'm True to the Navy Now" (King-Janis); "Sweeping the Clouds Away" (Sam Coslow)

Released: April 1930; 102 minutes

Following *The Hollywood Revue of 1929* and *The Show of Shows*, *Paramount on Parade* offers a variety show parading the studio's most lustrous stars. Capitalizing on their screen images, William Powell is seen as detective Philo Vance, Warner Oland as Fu Manchu, Maurice Chevalier (directed by Ernst Lubitsch) doing an Apache dance with Evelyn Brent, Clara Bow in a nautical number, Helen Kane as a Boop-Boop-a-Dooping school teacher, Ruth Chatterton as a teary Montmartre street walker, and Chevalier leading a chorus of chimney sweeps across the roofs of Paris and eventually up on a rainbow. Paramount utilized no less than 11 directors on this project, which was also released in French and Spanish versions with Jeanette MacDonald as mistress of ceremonies.

Anytime's the Time to Fall in Love

FROM PARAMOUNT ON PARADE

Words by ELSIE JANIS
Music by JACK KING

Why do you keep on stall - ing when I'm call - ing ev - 'ry

Copyright © 1930 (Renewed) 1957 by Famous Music Corporation
International Copyright Secured   All Rights Reserved

THE SMILING LIEUTENANT

Music: Oscar Straus
Lyrics: Clifford Grey
Screenplay: Ernest Vajda, Samson Raphaelson, Ernst Lubitsch
Producer-director: Ernst Lubitsch for Paramount
Photography: George Folsey
Cast: Maurice Chevalier, Claudette Colbert, Miriam Hopkins, Charlie Ruggles, George Barbier, Hugh O'Connell, Elizabeth Patterson
Songs: "While Hearts Are Singing"; "Breakfast Table Love"; "One More Hour of Love"; "Jazz Up Your Lingerie"
Released: March 1931; 89 minutes

Maurice Chevalier and Claudette Colbert.

By 1931, the proliferation of musical films—there had been over 60 in 1930—became such a glut on the market that the public soon tired of them and no more than 15 were released during the year. Still, the Ernst Lubitsch-Maurice Chevalier formula continued to enjoy popularity, possibly because it broke so distinctively with the usual backstage fare and, during the dark days of the Depression, could be accepted as the purest kind of escapism. The spry and sprightly *Smiling Lieutenant* was based on a 1907 Oscar Straus Viennese operetta, *Ein Walzertraum* (A Waltz Dream), which had already been filmed as a German silent movie in 1925 with Mady Christians and Willy Fritsch. The story tells of flirtatious Lieutenant Niki (Chevalier) who so catches the eye and heart of drab, lovelorn Princess Anna (Miriam Hopkins) that—shades of *The Love Parade*—she chooses him for her prince consort. Although Niki has been having an affair with the vivacious Franzi (Claudette Colbert), the leader of an all-girl orchestra at an outdoor restaurant, she is well aware that their romance cannot last and even teaches Anna some of the tricks of love to keep Niki from smiling at anyone else. The film, which was shot at Paramount's Astoria, Long Island, studio, was also released in a French version called *Le Lieutenant Souriant*.

One More Hour of Love

FROM THE SMILING LIEUTENANT

Words by CLIFFORD GREY and OSCAR STAUS
Music by OSCAR STAUS

Copyright © 1931 (Renewed 1958) by Famous Music Corporation
International Copyright Secured   All Rights Reserved

Love Me Tonight

Music: Richard Rodgers
Lyrics: Lorenz Hart
Screenplay: Samuel Hoffenstein, Waldemar Young, George Marion Jr.
Producer-director: Rouben Mamoulian for Paramount
Photography: Victor Milner
Cast: Maurice Chevalier, Jeanette MacDonald, Charlie Ruggles, Charles Butterworth, Myrna Loy, C. Aubrey Smith, Elizabeth Patterson, Ethel Griffies, Blanche Friderici, Joseph Cawthorn, Robert Greig, Bert Roach, George "Gabby" Hayes, Tyler Brooke, Herbert Mundin, Cecil Cunningham, Marion "Peanuts" Byron, Rolfe Sedan, Edgar Norton, Rita Owin, Mel Calish
Songs: "That's the Song of Paree"; "Isn't It Romantic?"; "Lover"; "Mimi"; "A Woman Needs Something Like That"; "The Deer Hunt" (instrumental); "The Poor Apache"; "Love Me Tonight"; "The Son of a Gun Is Nothing but a Tailor"
Released: August 1932; 96 minutes

Tailor Maurice Chevalier sets out to deal with a money-owing customer.

With a title as dull as the picture itself was adventurous, *Love Me Tonight* was a seminal production in the evolution of a purely cinematic form of musical comedy. Through its close interweaving of plot, songs, background scoring, its imaginative camera work, and its skillful editing (by William Shea), it remains a timeless and constantly inventive creation. With Maurice Chevalier and Jeanette MacDonald in the leading roles, it is full of the deft, imaginative touches usually associated with the films of Ernst Lubitsch—only this time the director was, surprisingly, Rouben Mamoulian, whose work here contrasts strikingly with the melodramatic offerings (*Applause, Dr. Jekyll and Mr. Hyde*) with which he had previously been associated.

Mamoulian and Broadway songwriters Richard Rodgers and Lorenz Hart (who had written their first original Hollywood score in 1931 for *The Hot Heiress*) worked closely together to achieve the properly stylized blending of a fairytale story that was actually told through music. This they achieved through a number of remarkably staged sequences—the early morning opening scene showing Paris waking up to the sounds of the city (a concept the director borrowed from his own staging of the 1927 play Porgy and which would also be borrowed by director Otto Preminger for the 1959 film version of *Porgy and Bess*); the use of one song, "Isn't It Romantic?," to move the action from Maurice's tailor shop in Paris to Princess Jeanette's chateau in the French countryside; a deer hunt ballet in slow motion; a split-screen image of Chevalier and MacDonald who, though alone, seem to be singing the title song to each other; and the quick cutting to various parts of the chateau as the inhabitants register shock upon discovering that Chevalier, who has been masquerading as a baron, is nothing but a tailor. Another memorable scene shows the leading characters' first meeting on a country road (after Jeanette has sung "Lover" to her horse) in which Maurice expresses his confused romantic feelings in "Mimi".

Though Lubitsch was the obvious choice to direct *Love Me Tonight*, he was then working on *Trouble in Paradise* and Paramount studio head Adolph Zukor approached a reluctant Rouben Mamoulian to find a suitable vehicle for Chevalier and MacDonald. At the suggestion of playwright Leopold Marchand, he found the property in a play called *Tailor in the Chateau*, which Marchand had co-authored. One line from the film has since become a classic. After the lovelorn Princess Jeanette has had a fainting spell, Charlie Ruggles asks Myrna Loy, as the man-hungry Countess Valentine, if she could go for a doctor. "Certainly," she replies, "bring him right in."

Isn't It Romantic?

FROM THE PARAMOUNT PICTURE LOVE ME TONIGHT

Words by LORENZ HART
Music by RICHARD RODGERS

Calmly

I've nev-er met you, Yet nev-er
My face is glow-ing, I'm en-er-

doubt, dear, I can't for-get you, I've thought you out dear, I know your
get-ic, The art of sew-ing, I found po-et-ic, My nee-dle

pro-file and I know the way you kiss just the thing I
punc-tu-ates the rhy-thm of ro-mance! I don't give a

Copyright © 1932 (Renewed 1959) by Famous Music Corporation
International Copyright Secured All Rights Reserved

THE BIG BROADCAST

Screenplay: George Marion Jr.
Produced by: (uncredited) for
Paramount
Directed by: Frank Tuttle
Photography: George Folsey
Cast: Stuart Erwin, Bing Crosby, Leila
Hyams, Sharon Lynne, George Burns,
Gracie Allen, George Barbier, Eddie
Lang, Kate Smith, Boswell Sisters, Cab
Calloway Orch., Mills Brothers, Arthur
Tracy, Vincent Lopez Orch., Donald
Novis
Songs: "Dinah" (Harry Akst-Sam Lewis,
Joe Young); "Here Lies Love" (Ralph
Rainger-Leo Robin); "Please" (Rainger-
Robin); "Tiger Rag" (Nick La Rocca);
"Trees" (Oscar Rasbach-Joyce Kilmer);
"Crazy People" (James Monaco-Edgar
Leslie); "It Was So Beautiful" (Harry
Barris-Arthur Freed); "Kickin' the
Gong Around" (Harold Arlen-Ted
Koehler)
Released: October 1932; 78 minutes

The first of Paramount's four Big Broadcast movies set the pattern for the series by using a slim plot about broadcasting as an excuse to present an all-star lineup of musical talent. Thus we are offered the Mills Brothers harmonizing to "Tiger Rag", Cab Calloway gyrating through "Kickin' the Gong Around", Donald Novis singing his trademark "Trees", and Kate Smith filling both the screen and the soundtrack with "It Was So Beautiful". The tale, enlivened by some cinematic sight gags, is concerned with the rivalry between radio crooner Bing Crosby (his name in the picture) and wealthy Texan Stuart Erwin for the affection of Leila Hyams (Erwin gets her), and the problems arising when Crosby fails to show up on time for the Big Broadcast (though he does get to reprise "Please" for the finale). The movie credits a 1932 Broadway play, *Wild Waves*, as its source, but the only similarity was that it, too, was about a singer on a radio station.

Sountrak ST.

Dinah

FROM THE BIG BROADCAST

Words by SAM M. LEWIS and JOE YOUNG
Music by HARRY AKST

© 1925 MILLS MUSIC, INC.
© Renewed MORLEY MUSIC CO., B&G AKST PUBLISHING CO., and MILLS MUSIC, INC.
All Rights Reserved

Flying Down to Rio

Music: Vincent Youmans
Lyrics: Edward Eliscu & Gus Kahn
Screenplay: Cyril Hume, H. W. Hanemann, Erwin Gelsey
Produced by: Louis Brock for RKO Radio
Directed by: Thornton Freeland
Choreography: Dave Gould, Hermes Pan (Fred Astaire uncredited)
Photography: J. Roy Hunt
Cast: Dolores Del Rio, Gene Raymond, Raul Roulien, Ginger Rogers, Fred Astaire, Blanche Friderici, Franklin Pangborn, Eric Blore, Etta Moten, Betty Furness, Mary Kornman
Songs: "Music Makes Me"; "Carioca"; "Orchids in the Moonlight"; "Flying Down to Rio"
Released: December 1933; 89 minutes

Fred Astaire and Ginger Rogers play it cool after Fred has been thrown out of a Rio de Janeiro restaurant.

Though initially Fred Astaire's dancing partner in *Flying Down to Rio* was to have been Dorothy Jordan (wife of studio executive Merian C. Cooper), the film marked the first joint appearance of Astaire with Ginger Rogers (they did ten movies in all), whose dance to "Carioca" established the team. Created as a star vehicle for Dolores Del Rio, who was paired with Gene Raymond, the story is concerned with the daughter of a Rio de Janeiro hotel owner and the bandleader-songwriter-aviator who flies down to Rio to win her away from countryman Raul Roulien. As a climax, the film offers a spectacular aerial floorshow in which scantily clad chorus girls perform constricted dance maneuvers while strapped to the wings of airplanes. (The scene was later parodied in "The Riviera" sequence of Ken Russell's 1971 spoof, *The Boy Friend*.) The movie's most eyebrow-raising line (said by Mary Korman as a jealous North American friend of Miss Del Rio): "What have these South Americans got below the equator that we haven't?"

Classic InU. ST Turner VC.

1933

CARIOCA

FROM FLYING DOWN TO RIO

Words by GUS KAHN and EDWARD ELISCU
Music by VINCENT YOUMANS

© 1933 POLYGRAM INTERNATIONAL PUBLISHING, INC. (Renewed)
Rights for the Extended Renewal Term in the United States controlled by WB MUSIC CORP,
GILBERT KEYES MUSIC and LSQ MUSIC CO.
All Rights Reserved

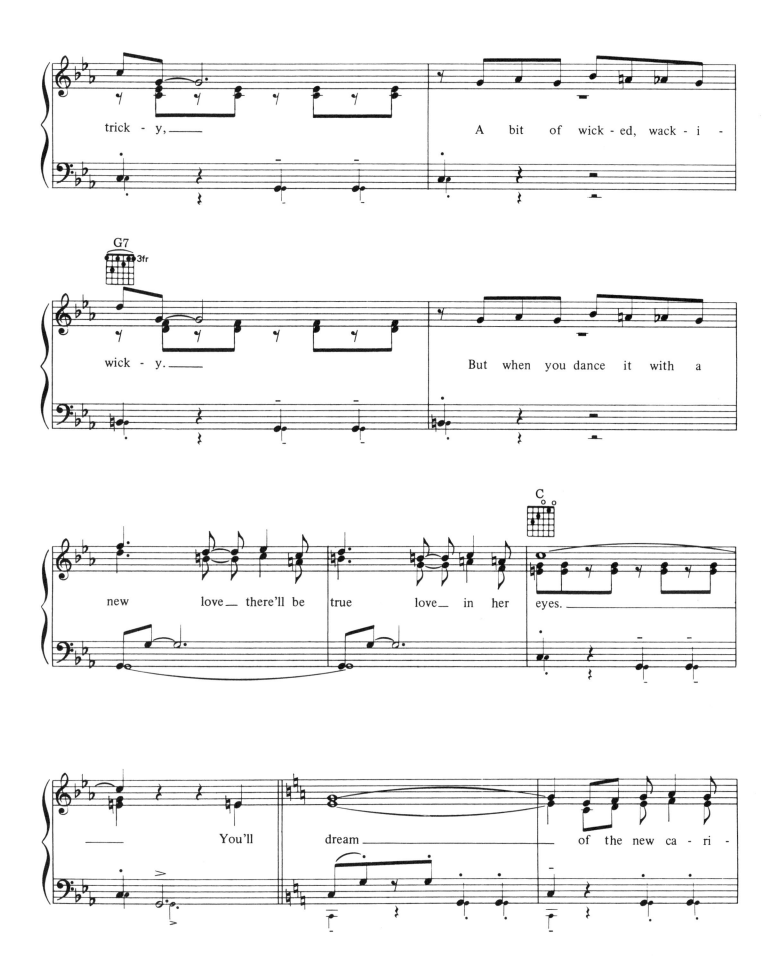

42ND STREET

Music: Harry Warren
Lyrics: Al Dubin
Screenplay: James Seymour, Rian James
Produced by: Darryl F. Zanuck for Warner Bros.
Directed by: Lloyd Bacon (Mervyn LeRoy uncredited)
Choreography: Busby Berkeley
Photography: Sol Polito
Cast: Warner Baxter, Bebe Daniels, George Brent, Ruby
Keeler, Dick Powell, Ginger Rogers, Una Merkel, Guy
Kibbee, Ned Sparks, George E. Stone, Allen Jenkins, Eddie
Nugent, Henry B. Walthall, Clarence Nordstrom, Harry
Warren, Al Dubin, Harry Akst, Jack LaRue, Louise Beavers,
Toby Wing, Dave O'Brien
Songs: "You're Getting to Be a Habit With Me"; "Shuffle Off to
Buffalo"; "Young and Healthy"; "Forty-Second Street"
Released: February 1933; 89 minutes

Director Warner Baxter has stern words for chorine Ruby Keeler. Looking on are Una Merkel, George E. Stone, and Ginger Rogers.

After only 11 film musicals released in 1932, there were well over 30 the following year. Just as the surge in 1929 could be credited to the success of the backstage musical *The Broadway Melody*, so the surge in 1933 could be credited to another backstage musical, the even more successful *42nd Street*. The movie's assets are its variety of characters, memorable songs, authentic backstage atmosphere, and wisecrack-peppered dialogue that is crisp and funny ("She only said no once, and then she didn't hear the question"). But its most notable innovations are the Busby Berkeley kaleidoscopic routines which made such imaginative use of the camera that they created their own fantasy world, one that would be impossible to achieve in any other entertainment medium.

Though the film was adapted from a novel by Bradford Ropes, there are marked variations in the story line and the characters. In the book, hard-driving director Julian Marsh is a wealthy homosexual who lives with juvenile lead Tommy Lawler, and Dorothy Brock, the aging star of Marsh's show Pretty Lady, is two-timed by her lover, Pat Denning. After Dorothy, while drunk, falls down a flight of stairs, Tommy recommends that Peggy Sawyer, a fresh-faced chorus girl from Maine, be given the chance to replace her. Overnight, Peggy becomes a first-magnitude star and a first-class bitch. On the screen, Marsh (Warner Baxter) is still hard-driving but now he's an ailing, chain-smoking loner who has been wiped out by the Wall Street crash. Dorothy (Bebe Daniels) and Pat (George Brent) are devoted to each other, and Tommy (Dick Powell) is smitten by blank-faced chorine Peggy (Ruby Keeler), just off the bus

from Sioux City, Iowa. When Dorothy gets drunk and breaks her ankle, the show's backer (Guy Kibbee) wants "Anytime Annie" Lowell (Ginger Rogers) to replace her, but Annie nobly recommends Peggy. On the opening night of the Philadelphia tryout (despite the movie's title, we never see the New York premiere), Marsh takes Peggy aside to give her a pep talk ending with classic line, "Sawyer, you're going out a youngster but you've got to come back a star." Pretty Lady, of course, is a smash (at least in Philadelphia).

The most elaborate Berkeley creations in the somewhat disjointed stage show are "Shuffle Off to Buffalo," in which a bridal couple takes a musical train ride, and the melodramatic "Forty-Second Street" finale, a panorama of the area with assorted types depicting the frantic, violent nature of that "naughty, bawdy, gaudy, sporty" locale. The film marked the screen debut of Ruby Keeler, who would be teamed with Dick Powell in six other Warners musicals.

In 1968, the Off-Broadway musical *Dames at Sea* was a partial spoof of the movie, as were two films, *The Boy Friend* (1971) and the Baxter's Beauties half of the two-part parody that made up *Movie, Movie* (1978). *42nd Street* itself was adapted in 1980 as a Broadway musical. It featured Tammy Grimes and Jerry Orbach and ran almost eight and one-half years.

MGM/UA VC.

Forty-Second Street

FROM 42ND STREET

Words by AL DUBIN
Music by HARRY WARREN

In the heart of lit-tle old New York, you'll find a thor-ough-fare. It's the part of lit-tle old New York that

© 1932 WARNER BROS. INC. (Renewed)
All Rights Reserved

44

Aline MacMahon, Joan Blondell, and Ruby Keeler react to the news that Dick Powell is backing their new show.

Gold Diggers of 1933

Music: Harry Warren
Lyrics: Al Dubin
Screenplay: Erwin Gelsey, James Seymour, David Boehm, Ben Markson
Produced by: Hal B. Wallis for Warner Bros.
Directed by: Mervyn LeRoy
Choreography: Busby Berkeley
Photography: Sol Polito
Cast: Warren William, Joan Blondell, Aline MacMahon, Ruby Keeler, Dick Powell, Ginger Rogers, Ned Sparks, Guy Kibbee, Clarence Nordstrom, Sterling Holloway, Ferdinand Gottschalk, Etta Moten, Billy Barty, Busby Berkeley, Dennis O'Keefe
Songs: "We're in the Money"; "Shadow Waltz"; "I've Got to Sing a Torch Song"; "Pettin' in the Park"; "Remember My Forgotten Man"
Released: May 1933; 96 minutes

So confident were the Warner brothers in the future of backstage musicals that preliminary work on *Gold Diggers of 1933* had begun even before 42nd Street was in general release. The new film was based on the same play (about a Boston Brahmin who falls in love with a chorus girl even though he suspects her of being a fortune hunter) that had led to previous Gold Diggers films in 1923 and 1929. Since the second, titled *Gold Diggers of Broadway*, also had songs, the studio found itself releasing two musicals within the space of four years that were both based on the same source.

In other respects, *Gold Diggers of 1933* was strongly linked to *42nd Street*. It retained the previous film's cast members Dick Powell, Ruby Keeler, Ginger Rogers, Ned Sparks, Guy Kibbee, and Clarence Nordstrom (George Brent was originally to play the Bostonian but he was replaced by Warren William), and it kept the same songwriters (Al Dubin had also written the lyrics for *Gold Diggers of Broadway*), co-author (James Seymour), costume designer (Orry-Kelly), music director (Leo Forbstein), and choreographer. That was the ubiquitous Busby Berkeley, who devised dazzling routines for such numbers as "Shadow Waltz" (girls in blonde wigs and white gowns appearing to play white electrified violins), "Pettin' in the Park" (almost a Freudian vision of New York's Central Park), and "Remember My Forgotten Man" (a panorama of post-war disillusionment). Also as in *42nd Street*—and as in *On With the Show* before that and in many a backstage musical to follow—an untried newcomer gets the chance to take over from a featured performer (in this case it's tyro songwriter Powell who replaces juvenile Nordstrom when he gets an attack of lumbago).

Possibly the element that distinguishes the 1933 Gold Diggers from other backstage sagas of the period is that it is the only one showing the influence of the Depression. In addition to the grim "Remember My Forgotten Man" sequence, the movie not only deals with the problems of raising money to produce a show, but also with the daily financial concerns of aspiring actresses Keeler, Rogers, Joan Blondell, and Aline MacMahon.

MGM/UA VC.

We're in the Money
(The Gold Diggers' Song)
FROM GOLD DIGGERS OF 1933

Words by AL DUBIN
Music by HARRY WARREN

© 1933 WARNER BROS. INC. (Renewed)
All Rights Reserved

She Done Him Wrong

Screenplay: Harvey Thew & John Bright, Mae West
Produced by: William LeBaron for Paramount
Directed by: Lowell Sherman
Photography: Charles Lang
Cast: Mae West, Cary Grant, Owen Moore, Gilbert
    Roland, Noah Beery, Rochelle Hudson, Fuzzy
    Knight, Grace LaRue, Louise Beavers
Songs: "Silver Threads Among the Gold" (Hart
    Danks-Eben Rexford); "Masie, My Pretty Daisy"
    (Ralph Rainger); "Easy Rider" (Shelton Brooks);
    "I Like a Guy What Takes His Time" (Rainger);
    "Frankie and Johnny" (trad.)
Released: February 1933; 66 minutes

Mae West's first starring vehicle was an adaptation of her own play, *Diamond Lil*, a Broadway success of 1928. Though Paramount was not optimistic about the film's prospects, it turned out to be one of the year's blockbusters with a domestic gross of over $2 million. The movie, which took only 18 days to shoot and runs for little over an hour, is set in New York's Bowery in the late 1890's. In the tale, saloon singer Lady Lou (changed from the original Lil) is involved in various shady dealings, including white slave traffic. She must also contend with a former lover who has just escaped from prison and a new love (Cary Grant, a federal agent disguised as a Salvation Army officer. The film was full of Miss West's characteristic one-liners (to an acquaintance who calls her a fine woman, she replies, "One of the finest women who ever walked the streets"), and also included the famous invitation to Grant, "Why don't you come up sometime 'n see me?"

MCA VC.

A Guy What Takes His Time

FROM *SHE DONE HIM WRONG*

Words and Music by
RALPH RAINGER

Copyright © 1932, 1933 (Renewed 1959, 1960) by Famous Music Corporation
International Copyright Secured   All Rights Reserved

The Cat and the Fiddle

Music: Jerome Kern
Lyrics: Otto Harbach
Screenplay: Bella & Samuel Spewack
Produced by: Bernard Hyman for MGM
Directed by: William K. Howard
Choreography: Albertina Rasch
Photography: Harold Rosson, Charles Clarke (part Technicolor)
Cast: Ramon Novarro, Jeanette MacDonald, Frank Morgan, Charles Butterworth, Jean Hersholt, Vivienne Segal, Joseph Cawthorn, Frank Conroy, Henry Armetta, Herman Bing, Sterling Holloway, Leonid Kinskey, Irene Franklin; Earl Oxford; Christian Rub
Songs: "The Night Was Made for Love"; "One Moment Alone"; "She Didn't Say 'Yes' "; "Don't Ask Us Not to Sing"; "I Watch the Love Parade"; "A New Love Is Old"; "Try to Forget"
Released: February 1934; 92 minutes

Jeanette MacDonald, Ramon Novarro

The Cat and the Fiddle was a rarity for its day in that every song in the original 1931 Jerome Kern-Otto Harbach stage production was retained for the movie version. Having gone this far, it is curious that the story should have been so altered. It's still the tale of American composer Shirley Sheridan (Jeanette MacDonald) who succumbs to the ardor of impetuous Rumanian composer Victor Flouescu (Ramon Novarro), a fellow student at the music conservatory in Brussels who has written an operetta. But on the screen most of the action is set in Paris and the new story is about the conflict that arises because Victor is unhappy being supported by Shirley, who has struck it rich by writing a hit song, "The Night Was Made for Love." (Victor had collaborated on the music but somehow he is not cut in on the royalties!) The film's climax, almost a satire on this sort of screen musical, has Shirley taking over the leading role in the operetta after Victor's patron and prima donna (Vivienne Segal) has left—even though Shirley has had nothing whatever to do with the production before opening night. Apart from the score, The Cat and the Fiddle was notable for its use of three color Technicolor for the final scenes of Victor's show.

H'wood Soundstage ST.

1934

A New Love Is Old

FROM THE CAT AND THE FIDDLE

Words by OTTO HARBACH
Music by JEROME KERN

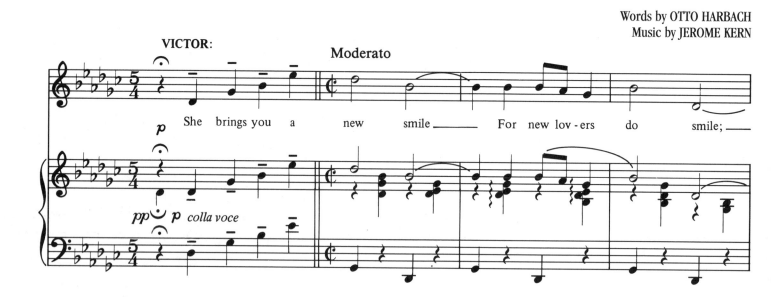

Copyright © 1932 PolyGram International Publishing, Inc.
Copyright Renewed
International Copyright Secured   All Rights Reserved

Take what she of-fers and be gay;

Love hates a man who runs a - way.

Hot, ea - ger lips can smoth-er

Thoughts, that re - call an-oth-er day. _____ She brings you a

p

p colla voce

molto espr.

new smile, _____ For new lov - ers do smile. _____

molto espr.

She tempts you and you smile; _____ A new love is told. _____ She brings you some new thrills, _____ Some ten - der and true thrills, _____ But af - ter a few thrills _____ Your new love is old. _____

THE GAY DIVORCEE

Screenplay: George Marion Jr., Dorothy Yost, Edward Kaufman
Produced by: Pandro S. Berman for RKO Radio
Directed by: Mark Sandrich
Choreography: Dave Gould, Hermes Pan (Fred Astaire uncredited)
Photography: David Abel
Cast: Fred Astaire, Ginger Rogers, Alice Brady, Edward Everett Horton, Erik Rhodes, Eric Blore, Betty Grable, Lillian Miles, E.E. Clive
Songs: "Don't Let It Bother You" (Harry Revel-Mack Gordon); "A Needle in a Haystack" (Con Conrad-Herb Magidson); "Let's K-nock K-nees" (Revel-Gordon); "Night and Day" (Cole Porter); "The Continental" (Conrad-Magidson)
Released: October 1934; 107 minutes

Betty Grable singing "Let's K-nock K-nees" to Edward Everett Horton.

Because the Hays office decreed that a divorce could never be gay but that a divorcee could, the title of the 1932 Broadway musical *Gay Divorce* had to be changed to *The Gay Divorcee* when RKO made the screen version with Fred Astaire (who had been in the original) and Ginger Rogers. The team's first starring vehicle, it also brought them together with director Mark Sandrich (who helmed five of their movies) and producer Pandro S. Berman (who was in charge of seven). Of Cole Porter's original stage score, the only song retained was "Night and Day," which served to introduce audiences to the sight of formally clad Astaire and Rogers performing the first of their romantic dance routines. Their skills on the dancefloor were further demonstrated through their introduction of the daring new dance sensation, "The Continental," in a sequence lasting 17 minutes.

In the story, dancer Guy Holden (Astaire) is mistakenly believed by divorce-seeking Mimi Glossop (Miss Rogers) to be the professional correspondent with whom she must spend the night at a fashionable English resort. Further complications arise when the real correspondent, Rodolfo Tonetti (Erik Rhodes repeating his stage role), shows up, but matters are pretty much straightened out by the next morning's breakfast.

1934

The Continental

FROM THE GAY DIVORCEE

Words by CON CONRAD
Music by HERBERT MAGIDSON

© Copyright 1934 (Renewed 1961) Magidson Music Company, Inc.
International Copyright Secured All Rights Reserved

THE MERRY WIDOW

Music: Franz Lehar
Lyrics: Lorenz Hart
Screenplay: Ernest Vajda & Samson Raphaelson
Produced by: Irving Thalberg for MGM
Directed by: Ernst Lubitsch
Choreography: Albertina Rasch
Photography: Oliver T. Marsh
Cast: Maurice Chevalier, Jeanette MacDonald, Edward Everett Horton, Una Merkel, George Barbier, Minna Gombell, Sterling Holloway, Donald Meek, Herman Bing, Henry Armetta, Akim Tamiroff, Shirley Ross, Leonid Kinskey, Richard Carle, Billy Gilbert, Virginia Field, Ferdinand Munier, Rolfe Sedan
Songs: "Girls, Girls, Girls"; "Vilia"; "Tonight Will Teach Me to Forget" (lyric: Gus Kahn); "Maxim's"; "Melody of Laughter"; "The Merry Widow Waltz"; "If Widows Are Rich"
Released: September 1934; 110 minutes

"The Merry Widow Waltz" preformed by Maurice Chevalier and Jeanette MacDonald at the Marshovian Embassy in Paris.

After director Ernst Lubitsch and his star attraction Maurice Chevalier had worked together on such operetta bonbons as *The Love Parade* and *The Smiling Lieutenant*, both at Paramount, it was almost inevitable that they would become involved in the first sound version of the most celebrated of all Viennese operettas, Franz Lehar's *The Merry Widow*. But since it was MGM, not Paramount, that held the rights, it was at that studio that the two men were brought together for their fifth and final association. Since he had already appeared in three films with Jeanette MacDonald, Chevalier wanted a change in his leading lady and fought to get the part for Grace Moore. Lubitsch, however, held out for Miss MacDonald. The movie also marks the only stage or screen assignment in which lyricist Lorenz Hart's words are not mated to the music of Richard Rodgers. (For contractual reasons, however, Rodgers received screen credit as co-lyricist.)

Based on a French play, *L'Attaché d'Ambassade*, the durable work had its premiere in 1905 (as *Die Lustige Witwe*), caused a sensation in London and New York two years later, and was screened twice in the U.S. as a silent—a 1912 two-reeler with Wallace Reid and Alma Rubens, and a much-altered Erich Von Stroheim feature-length adaptation in 1925 with John Gilbert and Mae Murray. For the 1934 *Merry Widow*, the action was set back from 1905 to the 1880's, the mythical kingdom's name was changed from Marsovia to Marshovia, Danilo was demoted from prince to count, widow Sonia Sadoya had lost her last name, and Marshovian Ambassador Popoff (Edward Everett Horton) no longer had an unfaithful wife. Most of the action takes place in Paris, where the dashing Danilo is on assignment from his government to woo and wed the wealthy widow to prevent her from marrying a foreigner. After mistaking Sonia for a cabaret girl at Maxim's (where another girl proudly exhibits a garter from Danilo inscribed "Many Happy Returns"), Danilo and Sonia meet again at the Marshovian Embassy ball. There, to the strains of the mesmeric "Merry Widow Waltz," they lead hundreds of waltzing couples as they airily glide through elegantly mirrored halls. Because Danilo's pride is hurt that Sonia considers him a fortune hunter, he refuses to fulfill his matrimonial mission and is tried and convicted in his homeland. Sonia then sets him free in the only way possible—she marries him.

A French version, *La Veuve Joyeuse*, shot by Lubitsch at the same time, also co-starred Chevalier and MacDonald. The third MGM remake of *The Merry Widow* was filmed in Technicolor in 1952 with non-singing Lana Turner (as Crystal Radek) and Ferdinand Lamas (as Count Danilo). Una Merkel, who played the queen in 1934, now showed up as Lana's best friend. To avoid confusion with this version, the 1934 *Merry Widow* has been given the meaningless title *The Lady Dances* when shown on television.

H'wood Soundstage ST. MGM/UA VC.

1934

The Merry Widow Waltz

FROM THE MERRY WIDOW

Words by ADRIAN ROSS
Music by FRANZ LEHAR

Gold — — en glow — — ing Lamps are

Copyright © 1993 by HAL LEONARD CORPORATION
International Copyright Secured   All Rights Reserved

GOLD DIGGERS OF 1935

Music: Harry Warren
Lyrics: Al Dubin
Screenplay: Manuel Seff & Peter Milne
Produced by: Robert Lord for Warner Bros.
Director-choreographer: Busby Berkeley
Photography: George Barnes
Cast: Dick Powell, Adolphe Menjou, Gloria Stuart, Alice
Brady, Glenda Farrell, Frank McHugh, Hugh Herbert,
Joseph Cawthorn, Grant Mitchell, Wini Shaw, Virginia Grey
Songs: "I'm Going Shopping With You"; "The Words Are in
My Heart"; "Lullaby of Broadway"
Released: March 1935; 95 minutes

The "Lullaby of Broadway" sequence with Wini Shaw and Dick Powell.

The first musical for which Busby Berkeley served as director as well as choreographer, *Gold Diggers of 1935* is distinguished primarily for two production numbers, "The Words Are in My Heart," featuring 56 girls supposedly playing 56 pianos, and especially "Lullaby of Broadway," a mini-morality musical. The latter, taking place in New York during a 24-hour dawn-to-dawn period, focuses on the hedonistic life of a girl-about-town (Wini Shaw), who sleeps all day and plays all night, and her playboy escort (Dick Powell). These two, it seems, are the only guests at a mammoth high-in-the-sky night spot where they are entertained by hundreds of frantically tapping dancers and where the girl is accidentally pushed to her death from a balcony. The film's chief gold digger is temperamental director Adolphe Menjou and the romance involves poor medical student Powell and rich non-singing, non-dancing Gloria Stuart.

MGM/UA VC.

1935

Lullaby of Broadway

FROM GOLD DIGGERS OF 1935

Words by AL DUBIN
Music by HARRY WARREN

© 1935 WARNER BROS. INC. (Renewed)
All Rights Reserved

MISSISSIPPI

Music: Richard Rodgers
Lyrics: Lorenz Hart
Screenplay: Francis Martin & Jack Cunningham
Produced by: Arthur Hornblow Jr. for Paramount
Directed by: A. Edward Sutherland
Photography: Charles Lang
Cast: Bing Crosby, W. C. Fields, Joan Bennett, Queenie Smith, Gail Patrick, Claude Gillingwater, John Miljan, Ann Sheridan, Dennis O'Keefe, King Baggott, Paul Hurst
Songs: "Roll Mississippi"; "Soon"; "Down by the River"; "It's Easy to Remember"; "Old Folks at Home" (Stephen Foster)
Released: April 1935; 73 minutes

Bing Crosby, King Baggott, W.C. Fields, and Paul Hurst.

Hollywood's second costume musical about a Mississippi showboat was based on Booth Tarkington's 1923 play, *Magnolia* (which had been filmed twice as a silent). It offers Bing Crosby as Tom Grayson, a peace-loving Philadelphian who refuses to follow the South's code of honor by fighting a duel over his fiancée (Gail Patrick). Branded a coward, Tom becomes a singer on a showboat run by Capt. Orlando Jackson (W. C. Fields), who publicizes him as "The Notorious Col. Steele." Eventually, Tom redeems his honor and ends in the arms of his former fiancée's sister (Joan Bennett). *Mississippi* had already begun shooting when leading man Lanny Ross was replaced by Crosby, who wanted another song. Since Rodgers and Hart had already returned to New York, they wrote the film's biggest hit, "It's Easy to Remember," while in the East, then sent a demo record to the producer. It is in this movie that Fields, relating the tale of his battle against the savage Indian, mutters the deathless line, "I unsheathed my Bowie knife and cut a path through this wa-a-all of human flesh dragging my canoe behind me."

Decca (Crosby LP).

1935

It's Easy to Remember

FROM THE PARAMOUNT MOTION PICTURE MISSISSIPPI

Words by LORENZ HART
Music by RICHARD RODGERS

With you___ I owned the earth. With you___ I ruled cre - a - tion. No

you,___ and what's it worth? It's just an im - i - ta - tion.___

Slowly and expressively

Your sweet ex - pres - sion,___ the smile you gave me,___ the way you looked when we

Copyright © 1934, 1935 (Renewed 1961, 1962) by Famous Music Corporation
International Copyright Secured   All Rights Reserved

Top Hat

Music & lyrics: Irving Berlin
Screenplay: Dwight Taylor & Allan Scott
Produced by: Pandro S. Berman for RKO Radio
Directed by: Mark Sandrich
Choreography: Hermes Pan (Fred Astaire uncredited)
Photography: David Abel
Cast: Fred Astaire, Ginger Rogers, Edward Everett Horton, Helen Broderick, Erik Rhodes, Eric Blore, Lucille Ball, Leonard Mudie, Edgar Norton
Songs: "No Strings"; "Isn't This a Lovely Day?"; "Top Hat, White Tie and Tails"; "Cheek to Cheek"; "The Piccolino"
Released: August 1935; 101 minutes

Fred Astaire and male chorus in the "Top Hat, White Tie and Tails" number.

Since *The Gay Divorcee* had proved to be such an auspicious vehicle for Fred Astaire and Ginger Rogers in 1934, RKO used the same general formula the following year with *Top Hat*, a film that in style, plot, characterizations, and casting was so close to the previous movie that it amounted almost to self-plagiarism. The settings are again London and a fashionable resort (this time it's the Lido), and the wildly improbable tale of mistaken identity again finds Astaire as an American dancer falling in love at first sight with Rogers as another visiting American. The high points once more occur when the formally clad twosome appear on the dance floor both to reveal their love through a dance ("Cheek to Cheek," succeeding the previous film's "Night and Day") and to take part in an outdoor production number introducing a new melody ("The Piccolino," succeeding "The Continental"). The three male character comedians in *The Gay Divorcee*—Edward Everett Horton, Erik Rhodes, and Eric Blore—are again on hand to play, respectively, Astaire's prissy friend, Astaire's volatile rival, and Horton's bumptious valet. *Top Hat* also shared the same producer, director, choreographers, cameraman, art director (Van Nest Polglase), music director (Max Steiner), and editor (William Hamilton).

Generally regarded as the quintessential Astaire-Rogers musical, the film is further enhanced by a score by Irving Berlin (his first major Hollywood effort) consisting of five numbers all tied to situations in the plot. This is true even of Astaire's tailor-made "Top Hat, White Tie and Tails, " which, though seen as part of a London stage production, is performed in a way that makes the song's "invitation through the mails" refer to a telegram Horton had received from his wife (Helen Broderick) in the previous scene. (The number's climax with Astaire shooting down chorus boys with his cane was based on a routine the dancer had performed in the 1930 stage musical, *Smiles*.) One logic-stretching period covers a single night at the Lido resort that includes the cheek-to-cheek dance, a marital misunderstanding, a phony wedding, a threatened duel, a gondola drifting out to sea, and the elaborate "Piccolino" finale (which presumably takes place at dawn).

Director Mark Sandrich began work on *Top Hat* in December 1934, some four months before actual shooting, and Astaire devoted at least five weeks to blocking out and rehearsing the dance numbers. Making a brief appearance in a flower shop scene was Lucille Ball who, in 1958, would take control of the RKO Radio studio for her own television company, Desilu Productions. The chief mishap that occurred during filming involved the gown Ginger Rogers wore in the "Cheek to Cheek" sequence. The dress was covered with thousands of feathers and as Ginger began to dance the feathers began to molt. Dozens of takes were required before the dance was finally completed without any of the flying tufts visible on the screen. This scene was used again as the climax to Woody Allen's 1985 film *The Purple Rose of Cairo*.

Columbia (Astaire CD); Sountrak ST. Turner VC.

Isn't This a Lovely Day
(To Be Caught in the Rain?)
FROM THE RKO Radio Motion Picture TOP HAT

Words and Music by
IRVING BERLIN

© Copyright 1935 by Irving Berlin
Copyright Renewed
International Copyright Secured   All Rights Reserved

ROBERTA

Music: Jerome Kern
Lyrics: Otto Harbach*; Dorothy Fields **
Screenplay: Jane Murfin, Sam Mintz, Glen Tryon, Allan Scott
Produced by: Pandro S. Berman for RKO Radio
Directed by: William A. Seiter
Choreography: Hermes Pan (Fred Astaire uncredited)
Photography: Edward Cronjager
Cast: Irene Dunne, Fred Astaire, Ginger Rogers, Randolph Scott, Helen Westley, Victor Varconi, Claire Dodd, Lucille Ball, Candy Candido, Gene Sheldon
Songs: "Let's Begin"*; "I'll Be Hard to Handle" (lyric: Bernard Dougall); "Yesterdays"*; "I Won't Dance"** (lyric with Oscar Hammerstein II); "Smoke Gets in Your Eyes"*; "Lovely to Look At"**
Released: February 1935; 105 minutes

Ginger Rogers and Fred Astaire dancing to "Smoke Gets in Your Eyes."

Kern and Harbach's *Roberta* gave RKO the opportunity to star the established Irene Dunne with the popular new team of Fred Astaire and Ginger Rogers. The movie was adapted from a 1933 Broadway musical that had been based on Alice Duer Miller's novel *Gowns by Roberta*, but it made sure to build up the Astaire and Rogers parts and it added two pieces, "I Won't Dance" (for a dazzling Astaire solo) and "Lovely to Look At" (the theme of the fashion show that concludes the film), to the four songs retained from the stage production. The story relates what happens when former All-American halfback John Kent (Randolph Scott) inherits his Aunt Minnie's Parisian haute couture establishment, Roberta's, and falls in love with his aunt's assistant, exiled Russian Princess Stephanie (Miss Dunne). The new secondary plot concerns John's friend Huck Haines (Astaire), band-leader of the Wabash Indianians, and his rather casual romance with hometown girlfriend Lizzie Gatz (Miss Rogers), now singing at the Cafe Russe under the name of Countess Tanka Scharwenka. This, of course, is just an excuse for the team to light up the screen with their dances to "I'll Be Hard to Handle" and "Smoke Gets in Your Eyes." A second screen version of *Roberta*, called *Lovely to Look At*, was released in 1952 (see page 172).

Classic Intl. ST. MGM/UA VC.

Smoke Gets in Your Eyes

FROM ROBERTA

Words by OTTO HARBACH
Music by JEROME KERN

Copyright © 1933 PolyGram International Publishing, Inc.
Copyright Renewed
International Copyright Secured All Rights Reserved

ANYTHING GOES

Music & lyrics: Cole Porter, etc.
Screenplay: Howard Lindsay, Russel Crouse, Guy Bolton
Produced by: Benjamin Glazer for Paramount
Directed by: Lewis Milestone
Photography: Karl Struss
Cast: Bing Crosby, Ethel Merman, Charlie Ruggles, Ida Lupino, Arthur Treacher, Grace Bradley, Richard Carle, Margaret Dumont, Philip Ahn, Keye Luke, Dennis O'Keefe, Chill Wills
Songs: "Anything Goes"; "I Get a Kick Out of You"; There'll Always Be a Lady Fair"; "Sailor Beware" (Richard Whiting-Leo Robin); Moonburn" (Hoagy Carmichael-Edward Heyman); "My Heart and I" (Frederick Hollander-Robin); "You're the Top"; "Shanghai-Di-Ho" (Hollander-Robin)
Released: February 1936; 92 minutes

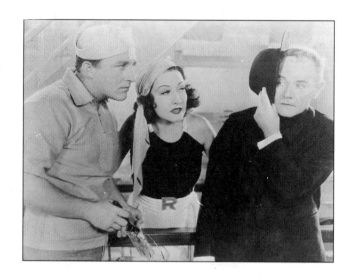

Bing Crosby, Ethel Merman, and Charlie Ruggles.

On Broadway, where it opened in 1934, *Anything Goes* was one of the decade's merriest and most successful musicals. The movie version enlisted three of the four original writers, kept four of the original 12 Cole Porter songs (though there were changes in the lyric to "You're the Top"), and retained Ethel Merman to repeat her role of Reno Sweeney, a nightclub singer sailing on an ocean liner from New York to Southampton. Otherwise, four new numbers were added (including "Moonburn," Hoagy Carmichael's first movie song), energetic William Gaxton was replaced by easygoing Bing Crosby and bumbling Victor Moore by bumbling Charlie Ruggles (who took over from W. C. Fields). In the story, Billy Crocker (Crosby), a friend of Reno's, stows aboard the ship to be near Hope Harcourt (Ida Lupino), the heiress he loves, and Public Enemy No. 13 (Ruggles) masquerades as the Rev. Dr. Moon. Eventually, Reno snares a titled Englishman (Arthur Treacher), Billy gets his Hope, and Dr. Moon is officially declared harmless.

In 1956, Paramount released a second film titled *Anything Goes*, but it bore scant relationship to the first except that Crosby was also in it and five of the original Porter songs were used (James Van Heusen and Sammy Cahn came up with three new ones). Jeanmaire, Mitzi Gaynor, and Donald O'Connor were co-starred. For its showings on television, the original *Anything Goes* has been given the awkward title *Tops is the Limit*. Decca (Crosby LP).

I Get a Kick Out of You

FROM ANYTHING GOES

Words and Music by
COLE PORTER

© 1934 WARNER BROS. INC. (Renewed)
All Rights Reserved

Born to Dance

Music & lyrics: Cole Porter
Screenplay: Jack McGowan & Sid Silvers
Produced by: Jack Cummings for MGM
Directed by: Roy Del Ruth
Choreography: Dave Gould
Photography: Ray June
Cast: Eleanor Powell, James Stewart, Virginia Bruce, Una
    Merkel, Sid Silvers, Frances Langford, Raymond Walburn,
    Alan Dinehart, Buddy Ebsen, Juanita Quigley,
    Georges & Jalna, Reginald Gardiner, Barnett Parker, The
    Foursome, Helen Troy, Dennis O'Keefe, Roger Edens
Songs: "Rolling Home"; Rap Tap on Wood"; "Hey, Babe, Hey";
    "Entrance of Lucy James"; "Love Me Love My Pekinese"; "Easy to
    Love"; "I've Got You Under My Skin"; Swingin' the Jinx Away"
Released: November 1936; 105 minutes

**"Hey, Babe, Hey" performed at the Lonely Hearts Club by Frances
Langford, Buddy Ebsen, Eleanor Powell, James Stewart, Una
Merkel, and Sid Silvers.**

Cole Porter went to Hollywood late in 1935 under contract to MGM to write his first screen score. After tossing ideas around for two months, writers Jack McGowan and Sid Silvers came up with a story, originally called *Great Guns!*, about three sailors (to be played by Allan Jones, Buddy Ebsen, and Silvers) on assignment in New York who become romantically involved with three hostesses (Eleanor Powell, Judy Garland, and Una Merkel) at the Lonely Hearts Club. For conflict, a bored socialite (Frances Langford) was added to try to win Jones away from Powell. As the work progressed, Jones was replaced by James Stewart (who thereby got to introduce "Easy to Love," performed in a Central Park setting), Miss Garland by Miss Langford, and Miss Langford by Virginia Bruce, whose role was changed to that of a tempestuous musical-comedy star. Along the way, three numbers were dropped: "Goodbye, Little Dream, Goodbye," "It's De-Lovely," and "Who but You?"

In the tradition of backstage movies, the inexperienced Miss Powell gets to replace Miss Bruce in a new Broadway show, even though one is a tall, leggy, dark-haired dancer and the other a slim, delicate featured blonde singer. Sonja Henie was to have made her screen debut in *Born to Dance* but her fee of $100,000 for two minutes of figure skating was considered a bit too much. Therefore, instead of Jimmy taking Virginia to an ice-skating rink, they go to the more formal Club Continental to see Georges and Jalna dance to "I've Got You Under My Skin" (later sung by Miss Bruce to Stewart on a mammoth penthouse terrace).

The movie's spectacular climax, "Swingin' the Jinx Away," was performed as the finale of a nautical revue during its opening night on Broadway. The scene is the forward portion of a battleship on which Captain Eleanor, wearing shako, black cape and spangled tights, taps and turns cartwheels in front of a crew of thousands of dancing sailors and a blaring military band.

Released the year between two Broadway Melody musicals, *Born to Dance* was really Broadway Melody of 1937 under another name. All three movies have the same female tapping star, along with the same comic dancer (Ebsen), director (Roy Del Ruth), writers (McGowan and Silvers), choreographer (Dave Gould), orchestrator (Roger Edens), art director (Cedric Gibbons), costume designer (Adrian), and editor (Blanche Sewell). And all three were concerned with what it takes for an inexperienced dancer to win the leading role in her very first Broadway musical.

Classic Intl. ST. MGM/UA VC.

I've Got You Under My Skin

FROM BORN TO DANCE

Words and Music by
COLE PORTER

Copyright © 1936 by Chappell & Co.
Copyright Renewed, Assigned to John F. Wharton, Trustee of the Cole Porter Musical and Literary Property Trusts
Chappell & Co. owner of publication and allied rights throughout the world
International Copyright Secured   All Rights Reserved

FOLLOW THE FLEET

Music & lyrics: Irving Berlin
Screenplay: Dwight Taylor & Allan Scott
Produced by: Pandro S. Berman for RKO Radio
Directed by: Mark Sandrich
Choreography: Hermes Pan (Fred Astaire uncredited)
Photography: David Abel
Cast: Fred Astaire, Ginger Rogers, Randolph Scott,
Harriet Hilliard, Astrid Allwyn, Lucille Ball, Betty
Grable, Joy Hodges, Tony Martin, Frank Jenks, Ray
Mayer, Russell Hicks, Harry Beresford, Addison
Randall, Herbert Rawlinson
Songs: "We Saw the Sea"; "Let Yourself Go"; "Get Thee
Behind Me, Satan"; "I'd Rather Lead a Band"; "But
Where Are You?"; "I'm Putting All My Eggs in One
Basket"; "Let's Face the Music and Dance"
Released: February 1936; 110 minutes

After putting Fred Astaire and Ginger Rogers in the elegant surroundings of *The Gay Divorcee, Roberta,* and *Top Hat,* producer Pandro Berman felt that it was time to lower their social standing. To achieve this, he cast them in a musical loosely based on a 1922 Broadway play, *Shore Leave* by Hubert Osborne, which was about Connie Martin, a New England dressmaker, who becomes so smitten with Bilge Smith, a marriage-shy sailor, that she has a ship salvaged for him after his discharge. Berman, of course, was well aware that the play, which was filmed in 1925, had also served as the basis for a 1927 musical comedy, *Hit the Deck* (score by Vincent Youmans, Clifford Grey, and Leo Robin), which RKO turned into a movie three years later with Jack Oakie and Polly Walker. This time, however, the producer wanted an entirely new approach. Thus, in *Follow the Fleet,* with Randolph Scott as Bilge and Harriet Hilliard as Connie, their story became secondary to one involving two newly created characters: sailor Bake Baker, Bilge's shipmate, and dancehall singer Sherry Martin, Connie's sister, a former vaudeville team who meet again at the Paradise Ballroom in San Francisco. For the score, though the RKO brass favored Harry Warren and Al Dubin, Berman insisted on retaining Irving Berlin, whose songs had proved so important to the success of *Top Hat,* the last Fred and Ginger vehicle.

As Bake and Sherry, Astaire and Rogers provided a contrasting comic romance just as they had previously done in *Roberta* (in which Scott had also played Astaire's friend), thereby replacing the customary character comedians who had given such valuable support in all previous Astaire-Rogers movies. The film's main locales were the dancehall (where the partners let themselves go dancing to "Let Yourself Go"), the deck of a battleship (where Astaire leads the tapping sailors in

Astaire and Rogers in the glamorous finale of "Let's Face the Music and Dance."

"I'd Rather Lead a Band"), and the deck of a reconstructed steam schooner (where Fred and Ginger clown around rehearsing "I'm Putting All My Eggs in One Basket" and later perform the compelling "Let's Face the Music and Dance" as part of a benefit show). In 1981, the last sequence was inserted in Herbert Ross's film, *Pennies from Heaven.* Two Berlin songs, "Moonlight Maneuvers" and "With a Smile on My Face," though written for *Follow the Fleet,* were never used in the movie.

Seen briefly in *Follow the Fleet* were sailor Tony Martin (in his film debut), backup singer Betty Grable, and Lucille Ball as one of the Paradise girls. (After a burly, gravel-voiced sailor makes a pass at her, Lucille deadpans, "Tell me, little boy, did you get a whistle or a baseball bat with that suit?")

Matching the popularity of the previous year's *Roberta* and *Top Hat,* *Follow the Fleet* turned out to be one of the biggest box office winners of 1936.

Columbia (Astaire CD); H'wood Soundstage ST. Turner VC.

Let Yourself Go

FROM THE MOTION PICTURE FOLLOW THE FLEET

Words and Music by
IRVING BERLIN

© Copyright 1936 by Irving Berlin
Copyright Renewed
International Copyright Secured All Rights Reserved

The Great Ziegfeld

Music: Walter Donaldson, etc.
Lyrics: Harold Adamson, etc.
Screenplay: William Anthony McGuire
Produced by: Hunt Stromberg for MGM
Directed by: Robert Z. Leonard
Choreography: Seymour Felix
Photography: Oliver T. Marsh, George Folsey, Karl Freund, Ray June
Cast: William Powell, Myrna Loy, Luise Rainer, Frank Morgan, Fanny Brice, Virginia Bruce, Reginald Owen, Ray Bolger, Ernest Cossart, Joseph Cawthorn, Nat Pendleton, Harriet Hoctor, Herman Bing, Raymond Walburn, William Demarest, Dennis Morgan, Virginia Grey, Jean Chatburn, A.A. Trimble, Buddy Doyle, Esther Muir, Robert Greig, Charles Judels
Songs: "Won't You Come and Play With Me?" (Anna Held); "It's Delightful to Be Married" (Vincent Scotto-Held); "If You Knew Susie" (Joseph Meyer-B.G. DeSylva); "Shine on Harvest Moon" (Nora Bayes-Jack Norworth); "A Pretty Girl Is Like a Melody" (Irving Berlin); "You Gotta Pull Strings"; "She's a Follies Girl"; "You"; "You Never Looked So Beautiful"; "Queen of the Jungle"; "My Man" (Maurice Yvain-Channing Pollock); "A Circus Must Be Different in a Ziegfeld Show" (Con Conrad-Herb Magidson)
Released: April 1936; 176 minutes

The "Pretty Girl Is Like a Melody" number, with Virginia Bruce atop the volute.

Broadway's legendary showman, Florenz Ziegfeld, produced 52 musicals between 1896 and 1931, including 21 editions of the opulent *Ziegfeld Follies*, plus such book shows as *Sally*, *Rio Flita*, *Show Boat*, *Rosalie*, *The Three Musketeers*, and *Whoopee*. *The Great Ziegfeld*, the first of a number of elaborate show-business screen biographies, purports to trace Ziegfeld's career from the days he managed Sandow the Strong Man at the Chicago World's Fair of 1893, through his stage successes, financial reverses, relationships with his two wives (the temperamental Anna Held and the more indulgent Billie Burke), and death at the age of 65. William Powell portrays the craggy, bilious impresario as a witty, urbane charmer but it is Luise Rainer as Anna who has the film's most memorable dramatic scene in which she makes an hysterical telephone call to her former husband congratulating him on his new marriage.

The most memorable musical scene, supposedly taking place during the first *Ziegfeld Follies*, was built around the song "A Pretty Girl Is Like a Melody" (which Irving Berlin had written for the 13th annual edition in 1919). Added as an afterthought and costing a record $220,000, the scene features a towering volute, 70 feet in diameter, with 175 spiral steps and weighing 100 tons. As the structure revolves, Dennis Morgan (unaccountably dubbed by Allan Jones) sings the theme song, with some 82 singers, dancers, and musicians performing selections ranging from *Pagliacci* to the *Rhapsody in Blue*. The sequence ends with the sight of

Virginia Bruce, as the Spirit of the Follies, perched atop the volute as a satin curtain descends in folds all around it.

Ziegfeld's associates, librettist William Anthony McGuire, had first sold the idea of a biographical film to Universal, but the studio abandoned the project after a year, and MGM secured the rights. At first the cast was to have included such Ziegfeld luminaries as Marilyn Miller, Irving Berlin, Gilda Grey, Ann Pennington, and Leon Errol, but they either refused to appear in the movie or were left on the cutting-room floor. Two discoveries, Eddie Cantor and Will Rogers, were impersonated by, respectively, Buddy Doyle and A. A. Trimble. The movie did, however, feature two authentic Ziegfeld attractions: comedienne Fanny Brice (whose specialty, "My Man," was unconscionably abridged) and contortionistic ballet dancer Harriet Hoctor. One alleged discovery, Ray Bolger, had never been in a Ziegfeld show. Ziegfeld was again played by Powell in the 1946 film, *Ziegfeld Follies*; others who portrayed him on the screen were Paul Henreid in *Deep in My Heart* (1954) and Walter Pidgeon in *Funny Girl* (1968).

Classic Intl. ST. MGM/UA VC.

1936

A Pretty Girl Is Like a Melody

FROM THE GREAT ZIEGFELD

Words and Music by
IRVING BERLIN

© Copyright 1919 by Irving Berlin
Copyright Renewed
International Copyright Secured   All Rights Reserved

Show Boat

Music: Jerome Kern
Lyrics & screenplay: Oscar Hammerstein II
Produced by: Carl Laemmle Jr. for Universal
Directed by: James Whale
Choreography: LeRoy Prinz
Photography: John Mescall, John Fulton
Cast: Irene Dunne, Allan Jones, Charles Winninger, Paul Robeson, Helen Morgan, Helen Westley, Donald Cook, Sammy White, Queenie Smith, Hattie McDaniel, Harry Barris, LeRoy Prinz, Eddie "Rochester" Anderson, Francis X. Mahoney, Sunnie O'Dea, Clarence Muse, Barbara Pepper, E.E. Clive
Songs: "Cotton Blossom"; "Where's the Mate for Me?"; "Make Believe"; "Ol' Man River"; "Can't Help Lovin' Dat Man"; "I Have the Room Above Her"; "Gallivantin' Around"; "You Are Love"; "Ah Still Suits Me"; "Bill" (lyric with P. G. Wodehouse); "Goodbye, My Lady Love" (Joe Howard); "After the Ball" (Charles K. Harris)
Released: April 1936; 113 minutes

The obviously smitten Irene Dunne and Allan Jones get differing reactions from Charles Winninger and Helen Westley.

Opening under the Ziegfeld banner in 1927, *Show Boat* was soon recognized as both a stage classic and a highly influential work in the development of the American musical theatre. The first screen version was adapted directly from the Edna Ferber novel on which the Kern-Hammerstein musical had been based. It was produced by Carly Laemmle for Universal in 1929, with Laura La Plante and Joseph Schildkraut in the leads. Though filmed as a silent, the movie was then reshot with some audible dialogue and songs, plus an 18 minute prologue featuring selections from the play sung by original cast members Helen Morgan, Jules Bledsoe, and Tess Gardella.

The 1936 screen version, produced by Laemmle's son, Carl Jr., was closer in spirit and design to the stage musical, with Hammerstein himself responsible for the adaptation. Nine of the original 16 songs were retained (incredibly, the duet, "Why Do I Love You?" was left on the cutting room floor), with three new ones—"I Have the Room Above," "Gallivantin' Around," and "Ah Still Suits Me"—written specially for the film. Heading the cast were Irene Dunne, who had played Magnolia Hawks in the original touring company, and Allan Jones, who had played Gaylord Ravenal in summer stock (though Laemmle's first choice had been Nelson Eddy). Helen Morgan (as the mulatto Julie LaVerne), Charles Winninger (as Magnolia's father and showboat owner, Captain Andy Hawks), and Sammy White (as hoofer Frank Schultz) were all veterans of the 1927 New York production. Paul Robeson, for whom the song "Ol' Man River" had been written, was in the London company in 1928 and on Broadway in the 1932 revival.

The episodic story covers the period from the mid-1880's to the present, and is concerned with the fortunes of the impressionable Magnolia Hawks and the ne'er-do-well riverboat gambler Gaylord Ravenal, who fall in love even before the first chorus of their first duet, "Make Believe." They become leading actors on the Mississippi showboat Cotton Palace (it had been Cotton Blossom on Broadway), get married, then take off for the high life in Chicago where their daughter Kim is born. Gaylord, however, soon loses his money and deserts his family. After Magnolia gets the chance to sing at the Trocadero nightclub on New Year's Eve (because the featured attraction, her old friend Julie, has obligingly walked out after singing "Bill" at a rehearsal), she has a tearful reunion with her father who helps her overcome her nervousness while singing "After the Ball." Eventually, both she and Kim become musical-comedy stars in New York. In the stage version, Magnolia and Gaylord are separated for 20 years and are reunited aboard the Cotton Blossom; in the 1936 film the reunion takes place not on the Mississippi, where it rightfully belongs, but in a Broadway theatre, where Ravenal is the backstage doorman, during the opening night of Kim's latest success.

MGM/UA VC.

Make Believe
FROM SHOW BOAT

Lyrics by OSCAR HAMMERSTEIN II
Music by JEROME KERN

The game of_ "just sup - pos - ing" is the sweet - est_ game I know,___

Our dreams are more ro - man - tic than the world we see.

Copyright © 1927 PolyGram International Publishing, Inc.
Copyright Renewed
International Copyright Secured   All Rights Reserved

1. We could do.

2. do.

3. last time do. Your par-don I pray, 'twas too much to say, The words that be - tray my heart. We on - ly pre - tend, You do not of - fend, In play-ing a lov - er's part.

a la Valse

smorzando

rall.

SWING TIME

Music: Jerome Kern
Lyrics: Dorothy Fields
Screenplay: Howard Lindsay & Allan Scott
Produced by: Pandro S. Berman for RKO Radio
Directed by: George Stevens
Choreography: Hermes Pan (Fred Astaire uncredited)
Photography: David Abel
Cast: Fred Astaire, Ginger Rogers, Victor Moore, Helen
Broderick, Eric Blore, Betty Furness, George Metaxa,
Landers Stevens, Frank Jenks, Ferdinand Munier, John
Harrington, Pierre Watkin, Gerald Hamer, Edgar Dearing
Songs: "Pick Yourself Up"; "The Way You Look Tonight";
"Waltz in Swing Time" (instrumental); "A Fine
Romance"; "Bojangles of Harlem"; "Never Gonna
Dance"
Released: August 1936; 103 minutes

Ginger Rogers and Fred Astaire dancing to the "Waltz in Swing Time."

Just as *Follow the Fleet* had previously lowered their social standing by making Fred Astaire a sailor and Ginger Rogers a dime-a-dance ballroom singer, so *Swing Time* (based on Erwin Gelsey's story, "Portrait of John Garnett") continued the process by making Fred a vaudeville hoofer and gambler and Ginger a dance instructress. It was the only Astaire-Rogers film directed by George Stevens (whose father, Landers Stevens, played Betty Furness's father in the movie), and it was their only one with a complete score by Jerome Kern and Dorothy Fields (though they had written two songs together for *Roberta*). The movie also gave the screen's premier male dancer the chance to perform some uncharacteristic routines: he was an inept dance pupil (but only as a joke, of course) at the beginning of "Pick Yourself Up," he wore blackface for the only time in his career in the "Bojangles of Harlem" number, and his wooing technique on the dancefloor failed to win over Ginger during their emotional performance of "Never Gonna Dance." Astaire even sang the chief romantic expression, "The Way You Look Tonight," in Ginger's hotel room while the object of his admiration was in the bathroom shampooing her hair.

Swing Time traces the rise of dancers Lucky Garnett and Penny Carrol at two elegant New York night clubs while at the same time dealing with romantic roadblocks caused by a society band leader (Georges Metaxa) in love with Penny and a small-town socialite (Betty Furness) to whom Lucky is engaged. The movie had its share of mind-boggling plot devices found in almost every Astaire-Rogers film, such as the one, early in the story, in which Lucky is persuaded by the members of his vaudeville dance act that, according to the latest fashion, he couldn't possibly get married wearing cuffless striped trousers with a cutaway. And then there is the scene at the Club Raymond where Lucky and Penny dance the "Waltz in Swing Time" as an audition for the Silver Sandal without anyone from the latter night club bothering to show up.

Swing Time also welcomed back the supporting comic characters that had been in two earlier Fred and Ginger vehicles, *The Gay Divorcee* and *Top Hat*, but had been dropped from *Follow the Fleet*: Helen Broderick as Penny's best friend, Victor Moore as Lucky's best friend, and Eric Blore in the truncated role of an officious dance-studio manager. Initially called *I Won't Dance*, then *Never Gonna Dance*, the movie scrapped such negative appellations in favor of the more upbeat *Swing Time*, even though the story had nothing to do with big bands or jitterbugs.

Columbia (Astaire CD); Sountrak ST. Turner VC.

The Way You Look Tonight
FROM SWING TIME

Words by DOROTHY FIELDS
Music by JEROME KERN

Andantino

mf

rall.

Eb   Cm   Ab   Fm7   Bb7   Eb

Some - day,   when I'm aw - f'ly low,   When the world is
love - ly,   With your smile so warm,   And your cheek so

mf

C7-9   Fm7   Bb7   Eb7

cold,   I will feel a glow just think - ing of   you
soft,   There is noth - ing for me but to love   you,

rall.   *f*

Ab   Fm7   Eb6   Bb7   Eb   Eb6   Fm   Bb   1. Eb   Eb6   Fm   Bb7

And the way you look to - night.
Just the way you look to - night._____   Oh, but you're

dim.   *mf* *a tempo*   *p*

Copyright © 1936 PolyGram International Publishing, Inc. and Aldi Music (c/o The Songwriters Guild Of America)
Copyright Renewed
International Copyright Secured   All Rights Reserved

Alice Faye "Slumming on Park Avenue."

ON THE AVENUE

Music & lyrics: Irving Berlin
Screenplay: Gene Markey & William Conselman
Produced by: Darryl F. Zanuck & Gene Markey for 20th Century-Fox
Directed by: Roy Del Ruth
Choreography: Seymour Felix
Photography: Lucien Andriot
Cast: Dick Powell, Madeleine Carroll, Alice Faye, Ritz Brothers,
George Barbier, Alan Mowbray, Cora Witherspoon, Walter Catlett,
Joan Davis, Stepin Fetchit, Sig Rumann, Billy Gilbert, Lynn Bari,
Marjorie Weaver, E. E. Clive
Songs: "He Ain't Got Rhythm"; "The Girl on the Police Gazette";
"You're Laughing at Me"; "This Year's Kisses"; "I've Got My Love to
Keep Me Warm"; "Slumming on Park Avenue"
Released: February 1937; 89 minutes

As something of a variation on the usual backstage musicals dealing
with the vicissitudes of getting a Broadway show ready for its
inevitably successful opening night, *On the Avenue* is about a
show—called *On the Avenue*—that is just beginning a lengthy run
on Broadway. Here the problem has to do with the efforts of Mimi
Caraway (Madeleine Carroll), the richest girl in the world, to stop Gary
Blake (Dick Powell), the show's star and author, from lampooning her
and her family so maliciously in one of the revue's sketches. Mimi and
Gary, of course, fall in love and manage to surmount the attempts of
Gary's jilted sweetheart and costar, Mona Merrick (Alice Faye), to drive a
wedge between the couple. Except for "You're Laughing at Me," sung by
Powell to Miss Carroll in Central Park, all the Irving Berlin songs are
introduced in scenes in the revue—including Miss Faye's torchy "This
Year's Kisses" and Powell's jaunty "I've Got My Love to Keep Me Warm."

On the Avenue was directly linked to the 1933 Broadway musical,
As Thousands Cheer, which also had a Berlin score and in which the
line, "On the avenue," was sung in the song "Easter Parade." That was a
satirical revue, created in the form of a newspaper, with all the scenes
commenting on newsworthy people and events. In effect, the movie's plot
tells what might have happened had one of the targets objected to the
way he or she was depicted in the show.

H'wood Soundstage ST.

I've Got My Love to Keep Me Warm

FROM THE 20TH CENTURY FOX MOTION PICTURE ON THE AVENUE

Words and Music by
IRVING BERLIN

© Copyright 1936, 1937 by Irving Berlin
© Arrangement Copyright 1948 by Irving Berlin
Copyright Renewed
International Copyright Secured   All Rights Reserved

Snow White and the Seven Dwarfs

Music: Frank Churchill
Lyrics: Larry Morey
Screenplay: Ted Sears, Otto Englander, Earl Hurd, Dorothy Ann
   Blank, Richard Creedon, Dick Richard, Merrill de Maris, Webb Smith
Produced by: Walt Disney (released by RKO Radio)
Directed by: David Hand, Perce Pearce, Larry Morey, William
   Cottrell, Wilfred Jackson, Ben Sharpsteen (Technicolor)
Voices: Andriana Caselotti, Harry Stockwell, Lucille LaVerne, Roy
   Atwell, Pinto Colvig, Otis Harlan, Billy Gilbert, Scott Mattraw,
   Moroni Olsen
Songs: "I'm Wishing"; "One Song"; "With a Smile and a Song";
   "Whistle While You Work"; "Heigh-Ho"; "Isn't This a Silly Song?";
   "Some Day My Prince Will Come"
Released: December 1937; 83 minutes

Snow White with the dwarfs and enchanted animals.

It took a staff of over 750 artists working almost three years to create *Snow White and the Seven Dwarfs*, the screen's first feature-length cartoon. Walt Disney's trailblazing achievement also marked the first time human figures were animated (Marge Champion was the model for Snow White), but even more memorable was the humanizing and individualizing of the dwarfs (Doc, Grumpy, Happy, Sleepy, Sneezy, Bashful, and Dopey) and the vivid scenic designs, especially of the forest sequences, enhanced by Disney's initial use of three-color Technicolor and the special "multiplane" camera which gave the scenes a three-dimensional look.

Little Snow White, the fairy tale by Jacob and Wilhelm Grimm, underwent a number of changes on its way to the screen. In the movie, Snow White is considerably older than in the original story when the jealous Queen first tries to have her poisoned (in the book she had also tried strangling and paralyzing). In addition, Snow White is now brought back to life when the Prince kisses her (instead of when a poisoned apple is removed from her throat), and the Queen, disguised as a witch, now falls to her death in a ravine during a rainstorm (instead of dancing to her death in a pair of red-hot iron slippers at the wedding reception of Snow White and the Prince).

With a ticket sale of $6.7 million on its first release, *Snow White and the Seven Dwarfs* overtook the previous record of $4 million set by Al Jolson's *The Singing Fool* ten years earlier. In 1944, the RCA Victor recording of the Snow White score became the first soundtrack album of a motion picture. The film has been so successfully revived through the years that, as of 1989, it had grossed almost $62 million in U.S. and Canadian rentals and over $330 million worldwide. On July 17, 1987, in honor of the movie's 50th anniversary the film was re-released throughout the world. With 4,000 prints projected simultaneously in the United States and in 57 different countries, it was the biggest opening day in screen history.

Walt Disney began his career as a Hollywood film animator in 1923, but it was not until four years later that he created his most famous character, Mickey Mouse (known as Steamboat Willie in his first short subject with sound). Other popular animal cartoon characters conceived by Disney were Mickey's mate Minnie Mouse, Donald Duck, Goofy, Pluto the Pup, and the Three Little Pigs. Disney's only serious rivals at the time were Paramount's Dave and Max Fleischer, the inventors of Betty Boop, who, in 1939, released their own full-length cartoon feature based on Jonathan Swift's *Gulliver's Travels*.

The overwhelming success of *Snow White and the Seven Dwarfs* prompted Disney to make two other animated cartoons based on popular fairy tales, *Cinderella* (1950) and *The Sleeping Beauty* (1959), both of which have been periodically re-released. A fourth fairytale cartoon feature, *The Little Mermaid*, was made by the Disney studio in 1989. The following year, an animated sequel to Snow White called *Happily Ever After*, was released by Filmation.

RCA ST; Disneyland ST.

Someday My Prince Will Come

FROM SNOW WHITE AND THE SEVEN DWARFS

Words by LARRY MOREY
Music by FRANK CHURCHILL

Copyright © 1937 by Bourne Co.
Copyright Renewed
International Copyright Secured All Rights Reserved

ROSALIE

Music & lyrics: Cole Porter
Screenplay: William Anthony McGuire
Produced by: William Anthony McGuire for MGM
Directed by: W. S. Van Dyke
Choreography: Albertina Rasch
Photography: Oliver T. Marsh
Cast: Nelson Eddy, Eleanor Powell, Ray Bolger, Frank Morgan, Ilona Massey, Edna May Oliver, Billy Gilbert, Reginald Owen, George Zucco, Virginia Grey, William Demarest, Jerry Colonna, Al Shean, Janet Beecher, Pierre Watkin
Songs: "Who Knows?"; "I've a Strange New Rhythm in My Heart"; "Rosalie"; "In the Still of the Night"; "Spring Love Is in the Air"
Released: December 1937; 122 minutes

Eleanor Powell, surrounded by a chorus of thousands, dancing to the title song.

In 1928, librettist William Anthony McGuire took two recent events, Lindbergh's solo flight to Paris and the visit to the United States of Rumania's Queen Marie and her daughter, as his "inspiration" for a Broadway musical called *Rosalie*. Under Ziegfeld's sponsorship, it was turned into a sumptuously mounted vehicle for Marilyn Miller and became one of the successes of the season. For the screen version, MGM reversed its usual procedure: it retained the original story (McGuire was hired to write the screenplay and to produce the film) but scrapped the original score (divided between George Gershwin and Sigmund Romberg) in favor of a new one by Cole Porter. The result was a stupefying art-deco fantasy with a cast of literally thousands which managed to become one of the year's top moneymakers thanks to the odd pairing of its popular stars, Nelson Eddy and Eleanor Powell. It even produced two song hits, "Rosalie" (which the composer never liked) and the throbbing ballad, "In the Still of the Night." Frank Morgan, as the King of Romanza, was the only member of the cast who had been in the stage production.

In the Still of the Night

FROM ROSALIE

Words and Music by
COLE PORTER

Copyright © 1937 by Chappell & Co.
Copyright Renewed, Assigned to John F. Wharton, Trustee of the Cole Porter Musical and Literary Property Trusts
Chappell & Co. owner of publication and allied rights throughout the world
International Copyright Secured   All Rights Reserved

SHALL WE DANCE

Music: George Gershwin
Lyrics: Ira Gershwin
Screenplay: Allan Scott & Ernest Pagano
Produced by: Pandro S. Berman for RKO Radio
Directed by: Mark Sandrich
Choreography: Hermes Pan, Harry Losee (Fred Astaire uncredited)
Photography: David Abel
Cast: Fred Astaire, Ginger Rogers, Edward Everett Horton, Eric Blore, Jerome Cowan, Ketti Gallian, Harriet Hoctor, Ann Shoemaker, Ben Alexander, William Brisbane, Marek Windheim, Rolfe Sedan, Emma Young
Songs: "(I've Got) Beginner's Luck"; "Slap That Bass"; "Walking the Dog" (instrumental); "They All Laughed"; "Let's Call the Whole Thing Off"; "They Can't Take That Away from Me"; "Shall We Dance"
Released: April 1937; 116 minutes

Fred Astaire and Ginger Rogers' roller-skating dance to "Let's Call the Whole Thing Off."

While in Hollywood, Richard Rodgers and Lorenz Hart wrote a scenario for Fred Astaire in which they cast him as a dancer anxious to combine classical ballet with modern jazz. Astaire, however, rejected the idea since he felt his fans would not accept him in a role that gave him no opportunity to wear his trademark attire of top hat, white tie and tails. When the songwriters returned to New York they turned the story into a Broadway musical called *On Your Toes*, which became such a hit that it made Astaire change his mind. Producer Pandro Berman tried to secure the screen rights for an Astaire-Rogers vehicle, but lost out to Warner Bros., which incongruously teamed Eddie Albert and Vera Zorina. Nothing daunted, Berman went ahead with his own plans and came up with a story based on Lee Loeb and Harold Buchman's scenario called *Watch Your Step* that would also deal with the world of ballet.

In *Shall We Dance* (without the question mark), Astaire plays the part of Pete Peters, an American ballet dancer known as Petrov, who dreams of uniting classical movement with tap and ballroom dancing. While in Paris, Pete becomes smitten with American musical comedy star Linda Keene (Miss Rogers) and pursues and woos her (to "Beginner's Luck") on a palatial ocean liner heading for New York. Somehow the rumor gets around that they are secretly married, which prompts all sorts of naive misunderstandings and ludicrous plot complications after they land. Pete even gets the bright idea that, to put an end to speculation, they really do get married in order to get a divorce. (When Pete asks the officiating New Jersey judge what the grounds for divorce are in his state, the judge rasps the single word, "Marriage.") At the film's end—during an engagement at a swank rooftop nightclub—Pete fulfills his ambition to combine modern dancing with ballet, and, to no one's surprise, is also happily reunited with Linda.

The only Astaire-Rogers movie with a score by George and Ira Gershwin, *Shall We Dance* was the last of the team's vehicles to surround them with the kind of unrealistic luxury with which they were identified. It also surrounded them with their two most faithful supporting comedians, Edward Everett Horton as a fussy ballet impresario and Eric Blore as an unctuous hotel manager. Among the movie's highlights is the totally irrelevant musical logomachy, "Let's Call the Whole Thing Off," sung by Astaire and Rogers in Central Park, then danced to on roller skates. The number required four days of shooting and took less than two-and-one-half minutes on the screen.

At various times during its preparation, *Shall We Dance* was known as *Stepping Toes*, *Stepping Stones*, *Stepping High*, and *Watch Your Step*.

Columbia (Astaire CD); Sountrak ST. Tumer VC.

LET'S CALL THE WHOLE THING OFF

FROM SHALL WE DANCE

Music and Lyrics by GEORGE GERSHWIN
and IRA GERSHWIN

Moderately Fast

© 1936, 1937 (Renewed 1963, 1964) GEORGE GERSHWIN MUSIC and IRA GERSHWIN MUSIC
All rights administered by WB MUSIC CORP.
All Rights Reserved

ALEXANDER'S RAGTIME BAND

Music & lyrics: Irving Berlin
Screenplay: Kathryn Scola & Lamar Trotti
Produced by: Darryl F. Zanuck & Harry Joe Brown for 20th Century Fox
Directed by: Henry King
Choreography: Seymour Felix
Photography: J. Peverell Marley
Cast: Tyrone Power, Alice Faye, Don Ameche, Ethel Merman, Jack Haley, Helen Westley, Jean Hersholt, John Carradine, Wally Vernon, Ruth Terry, Dixie Dunbar, Grady Sutton, Chick Chandler, Tyler Brooke, Lon Chaney Jr., Robert Gleckler, Paul Hurst, Douglas Fowley, Cully Richards, Eddie Collins
Songs: "Alexander's Ragtime Band"; "Ragtime Violin"; "That International Rag"; "Everybody's Doin' It"; "Now It Can Be Told"; "This Is The Life"; "When the Midnight Choo-Choo Leaves for Alabam' "; "For Your Country and My Country"; "I Can Always Find a Little Sunshine in the YMCA"; "Oh, How I Hate to Get Up in the Morning"; "We're on Our Way to France"; "Say It With Music"; "A Pretty Girl Is Like a Melody"; "Blue Skies"; "Pack Up Your Sins and Go to the Devil"; "What'll I Do?"; "My Walking Stick"; "Remember"; "Everybody Step"; "All Alone"; "Easter Parade"; "Heat Wave"
Released: May 1938; 105 minutes

Jack Haley, Alice Faye, Don Ameche, Tyrone Power, and Wally Vernon.

*A*lexander's Ragtime Band was the first of a spate of movie musicals that sought to evoke nostalgia for the past through the songs of the past. In this case, all the songs were the creation of one man, Irving Berlin, with the story line merely a peg on which to hang 20 of his most familiar standards (plus two, "Now It Can Be Told" and "My Walking Stick," that were written specially for the film). Possibly because the leading character in the picture, like Berlin, was in charge of staging a revue during the first World War, there has been a mistaken belief that the movie is a biography of the songwriter. It is, in fact, a purely fictitious account covering the fortunes of a bandleader known as Alexander (Tyrone Power), his best friend Charlie Dwyer (Don Ameche), a pianist-composer, and singer Stella Kirby (Alice Faye), from their first meeting in a San Francisco honky tonk in 1911 (the year "Alexander's Ragtime Band" was written), through a variety of professional and personal ups and downs culminating in a glittering Carnegie Hall Concert in 1937 (doubtlessly prompted by Benny Goodman's concert the same year). Incredibly, not one of the characters ages a day during the 27 year period. The great appeal of the movie is in its ability of the familiar, changing rhythms of the songs—mostly sung by Miss Faye and Ethel Merman—to recreate the sense of time and atmosphere of the varying periods that are being covered in the episodic story.

The film, which cost over $2 million, required 85 sets, and was in preparation for over a year, had the same stars and director as another big-budget effort, *In Old Chicago*, which Fox had released earlier in 1938. It also inaugurated a period—roughly to the end of World War II—when the studio, under Darryl Zanuck, churned out a seemingly endless stream of costume musicals, biographical musicals, and picture postcard musicals almost invariably featuring at least one of Fox's stellar lineup of Alice Faye, Betty Grable, Sonja Henie, and Carmen Miranda.

The first of the Irving Berlin anthological surveys, *Alexander's Ragtime Band* led the way to Paramount's *Blue Skies* (1946), MGM's *Easter Parade* (1948), Paramount's *White Christmas* (1954), and 20th Century Fox's *There's No Business Like Show Business* (1954).

H'wood Soundstage ST

Alexander's Ragtime Band

FROM ALEXANDER'S RAGTIME BAND

Words and Music by
IRVING BERLIN

© Copyright 1911 by Irving Berlin
© Arrangement Copyright 1938 by Irving Berlin
Copyright Renewed
International Copyright Secured   All Rights Reserved

Big Broadcast of 1938

Music: Ralph Rainger
Lyrics: Leo Robin
Screenplay: Walter DeLeon, Francis Martin, Ken Englund
Produced by: Harlan Thompson for Paramount
Directed by: Mitchell Leisen
Choreography: LeRoy Prinz
Photography: Harry Fishbeck, Gordon Jennings
Cast: W. C. Fields, Bob Hope, Dorothy Lamour, Shirley Ross, Martha Raye, Lynne Overman, Leif Erickson, Ben Blue, Grace Bradley, Patricia Wilder, Shep Fields Orch., Tito Guizar, Kirsten Flagstad
Songs: "You Took the Words Right Out of My Heart"; "Brunnhilde's Battle Cry" (Wagner); "Thanks for the Memory"; "Mama, That Moon Is Here Again"; "The Waltz Lives On"
Released: February 1938; 90 minutes

Bob Hope and Shirley Ross at the railing of the Gigantic.

The fourth and final movie in Paramount's series celebrating radio entertainment benefited from the appearance of W.C. Fields (in the dual role of shipping magnate T. Frothingwell Bellows and his twin brother S. B. Bellows), who performed his classic routines on the golf course and at the billiard table. It also marked the feature film debut of a glib comedian named Bob Hope (who won the role after it had been turned down by Jack Benny). The movie, somewhat more elaborate than its predecessors, has a plot concerning a transatlantic race between two mammoth ocean liners, the Gigantic (where most of the action takes place) and the Colossal. To justify the movie's title—and the inclusion in the cast of such diverse talents as Shep Fields and His Rippling Rhythm, Mexican crooner Tito Guizar, and Wagnerian soprano Kirsten Flagstad—the Gigantic provides daily broadcasts presided over by Bob Hope. But the most memorable musical scene occurs at the ship's bar where Hope and Shirley Ross, as a still-in-love divorced couple, ruefully reminisce—in "Thanks for the Memory"—about the varied experiences they once shared.

Thanks for the Memory
From the Paramount Picture BIG BROADCAST OF 1938

Words and Music by LEO ROBIN
and RALPH RAINGER

Copyright © 1937 (Renewed 1964) by Paramount Music Corporation
International Copyright Secured   All Rights Reserved

CAREFREE

Music & lyrics: Irving Berlin
Screenplay: Ernest Pagano & Allan Scott
Produced by: Pandro S. Berman for RKO Radio
Directed by: Mark Sandrich
Choreography: Hermes Pan (Fred Astaire uncredited)
Photography: Robert de Grasse
Cast: Fred Astaire, Ginger Rogers, Ralph Bellamy, Luella Gear, Jack Carson, Clarence Kolb, Franklin Pangborn, Hattie McDaniel, Walter Kingsford, Kay Sutton
Songs: "I Used to Be Color Blind"; "The Yam"; "Change Partners"
Released: August 1938; 83 minutes

Fred and Ginger dance "The Yam."

Fred Astaire and Ginger Rogers' reunion movie found them surrounded by the trappings of believable affluence rather than by the implausible luxury of most of their previous vehicles. The first film in which Astaire did not play a dancer or a musician, *Carefree* cast him as a psychiatrist ("I wanted to be a dancer but psychiatry showed me I was wrong") whose dream-inducing treatment reveals that Miss Rogers is in love with him rather than with fiancé Ralph Bellamy. Surprisingly, considering that Irving Berlin wrote the songs, only three numbers are sung, with two others ("Since They Turned Loch Lomond Into Swing" and "The Night Is Filled with Music") played as orchestral accompaniment. The languorous "I Used to Be Color Blind" (written for a dream sequence originally planned in Technicolor) and the lively ballroom dance step "The Yam" (demonstrated at the exclusive Medwick Country Club) were the major Fred-and-Ginger dance routines. Astaire's golf dance, however, was his most original and difficult, combining harmonica playing, tap dancing, and golf-club swinging. To prepare for it, the dancer had to hit almost 1,000 balls during a ten-day rehearsal period that took two-and-one-half days to film. Total time on the screen: less than three minutes.

Classic Intl. ST.; Columbia (Astaire CD); Turner VC.

Change Partners

FROM THE RKO Radio Motion Picture CAREFREE

Words and Music by
IRVING BERLIN

© Copyright 1937, 1938 by Irving Berlin
Copyright Renewed
International Copyright Secured   All Rights Reserved

GOLDWYN FOLLIES

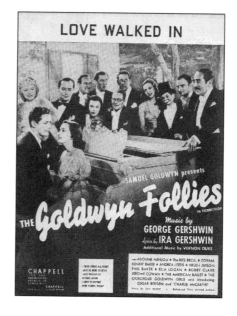

Music: George Gershwin
Lyrics: Ira Gershwin
Screenplay: Ben Hecht
Produced by: Samuel Goldwyn (released by United Artists)
Directed by: George Marshall
Choreography: George Balanchine
Photography: Gregg Toland (Technicolor)
Cast: Adolphe Menjou, Ritz Brothers, Edgar Bergen, Vera Zorina, Kenny Baker, Andrea Leeds, Helen Jepson, Phil Baker, Ella Logan, Bobby Clark, Jerome Cowan, Charles Kullman, Alan Ladd
Songs: "Love Walked In"; "Love Is Here to Stay"; "I Love to Rhyme"; "I Was Doing All Right"; "Spring Again" (music: Vernon Duke)
Released: January 1938; 120 minutes

After the death of Broadway impresario Florenz Ziegfeld in 1932, Hollywood impresario Samuel Goldwyn announced that he would carry on the *Ziegfeld Follies* tradition by producing his own annual *Goldwyn Follies*. Over the years at least nine successive writers were hired to work on what was to be the first in the series until, in 1937, Ben Hecht came up with something the producer liked. But despite such creative talents as the songwriting Gershwin brothers and choreographer George Balanchine, no one seemed to know what to do with a heterogeneous cast that included opera diva Helen Jepson, ballerina Vera Zorina, ventriloquist Edgar Bergen, and the Ritz Brothers (though partly because of its early use of three-color Technicolor, the picture showed up among the year's biggest box office hits). One of the innovations planned but never filmed was the screen's first full-length ballet, which was to have been choreographed to Gershwin's "An American in Paris." Because the composer died midway through the shooting (his last song was "Love Is Here to Stay"), Vernon Duke was assigned to write whatever additional music was needed.

Nelson VC.

1938

Love Is Here to Stay

FROM GOLDWYN FOLLIES

Music and Lyrics by GEORGE GERSHWIN
and IRA GERSHWIN

The more I read the pa-pers The less I com-pre-hend The world and all its ca-pers And how it all will end.

Noth-ing seems to be last-ing, But that is-n't our af-fair;

© 1938 (Renewed 1965) GEORGE GERSHWIN MUSIC and IRA GERSHWIN MUSIC
All rights administered by WB MUSIC CORP.
All Rights Reserved

Sweethearts

Music: Victor Herbert
Lyrics: Robert Wright & George Forrest
Screenplay: Dorothy Parker & Alan
  Campbell (Noel Langley uncredited)
Produced by: Hunt Stromberg for MGM
Directed by: W. S. Van Dyke
Choreography: Albertina Rasch
Photography: Oliver T. Marsh, Allen
  Davey (Technicolor)
Cast: Jeanette MacDonald, Nelson Eddy,
  Frank Morgan, Ray Bolger, Florence Rice, Mischa Auer, Terry
  Kilburn, Betty Jaynes, Douglas McPhail, Reginald Gardiner, Herman
  Bing, Allyn Joslyn, Raymond Walburn, George Barbier, Kathleen
  Lockhart, Gene Lockhart, Lucile Watson
Songs: "Wooden Shoes"; "Every Lover Must Meet His Fate";
  "Sweethearts"; "Pretty as a Picture"; "Summer Serenade"; "On
  Parade"
Released: December 1938; 114 minutes

Reginald Gardiner, Jeanette MacDonald, Nelson Eddy.

After a temporary split-up, Jeanette MacDonald and Nelson Eddy
resumed their partnership in *The Girl of the Golden West* and
Sweethearts, both released in 1938. The most lighthearted of their
movies, *Sweethearts*, marked the first time that the team gave up
period costumes or uniforms, and it was also MGM's first use of three-
color Technicolor. In most other respects, however, the film abides by
the usual formula of offering selections from a celebrated operetta score
(this one by Victor Herbert) while ignoring the original lyrics and story
(about a prince and princess in disguise that dated back to 1913). In the
film, MacDonald and Eddy appeared as costars of *Sweethearts*, a
Broadway hit still running after six years, who break up over a
misunderstanding but eventually get back together for what looks like at
least another six years. The couple made three more pictures together—
New Moon, *Bitter Sweet*, and *I Married an Angel*—but none was as
popular as their earlier efforts.

MGM/UA VC.

Sweethearts

FROM SWEETHEARTS

Words and Music by
VICTOR HERBERT

Copyright © 1994 by HAL LEONARD CORPORATION
International Copyright Secured   All Rights Reserved

but you real - ly must not mind it; If it comes not to your sigh - ing,

a tempo

there is al-ways one place you may find it; seek the dwell-ing of two hap - py sweet-hearts,

accel. *rit.*

pp

Tempo di Valse lente

you will find it there! _____ Sweet - hearts make love their

rit. *pp poco a poco in tempo*

ver - y own, sweet - hearts can live on

love a - lone, for them the eyes where love - light

lies o - pen the gates to Par - a -

dise! All oth - er love is doomed to

poco rit. *a tempo* *p*

fade, it is like sun - shine veiled in shade,

love their ver - y own, sweet - hearts can

live on love a - lone, for them the

eyes where love - light lies o - pen the

gates to Par - a - dise! All oth - er

poco rit.

BABES IN ARMS

Screenplay: Jack McGowan & Kay Van Riper (Noel Langley
uncredited)
Produced by: Arthur Freed for MGM
Director-choreographer: Busby Berkeley
Photography: Ray June
Cast: Mickey Rooney, Judy Garland, Charles Winninger, Guy Kibbee,
June Preisser, Grace Hayes, Betty Jaynes, Douglas McPhail, Rand
Brooks, John Sheffield, Henry Hull, Barnett Parker, Ann Shoemaker,
Margaret Hamilton, Charles Smith
Songs: "Good Morning" (Nacio Herb Brown-Arthur Freed); "You Are
My Lucky Star" (Brown-Freed); "Broadway Rhythm" (Brown-
Freed); "Babes in Arms" (Richard Rodgers-Lorenz Hart); "Where
or When" (Rodgers-Hart); "I Cried for You" (Gus Arnheim, Abe
Lyman-Freed); "Daddy Was a Minstrel Man" (Roger Edens); "I'm
Just Wild About Harry" (Eubie Blake-Noble Sissle); "God's Country"
(Harold Arlen-E. Y. Harburg)
Released: October 1939; 97 minutes

**As Mickey Rooney slaps the cello, Judy Garland and Betty Jaynes
sing their contrapuntal "Broadway Rhythm" and "You Are My Lucky
Star."**

On Broadway, where it opened in 1937, *Babes in Arms* was a small-
scale musical comedy which showed how some talented teenagers,
the children of former vaudevillians, manage to avoid being sent to
a work school by staging their own show. Though the screen version
retained the general outline of the plot, it kept only two of the original 11
Rodgers and Hart songs (among the casualties: "My Funny Valentine"
and "The Lady Is a Tramp"), changed the names of the characters, used
a minstrel show as the highlight of the revue, and added a romantic and
professional complication in the person of a Shirley Temple-type movie
star, played by tumbling June Preisser. It was also the first picture to
costar Mickey Rooney (who sang, danced, played piano and cello, and
imitated Clark Gable and Lionel Barrymore) and Judy Garland (whose "I
Cried for You" echoed her previous "Dear Mr. Gable"), and the first
product of the celebrated Freed Unit at MGM. Under the direction of
Busby Berkeley (his first at Metro), *Babes in Arms* succeeded so well—
distributors voted Rooney the most popular actor of the year—that it
spawned three other Mickey-Judy movies of the "Why don't-us-kids-put-
on-our-own-show" genre: *Strike Up the Band*, *Babes on Broadway*, and
Girl Crazy. It also begat such low-budget clones as MGM's *Born to Sing*
(1942) with Ray McDonald and Virginia Weidler (and a finale directed
by Busby Berkeley) and Universal's *Babes on Swing Street* (1944), with
Peggy Ryan, Ann Blyth, and even June Preisser.

Curtain Calls ST. MGM/UA VC.

1939

WHERE OR WHEN
FROM BABES IN ARMS

Words by LORENZ HART
Music by RICHARD RODGERS

Copyright © 1937 by Chappell & Co.
Copyright Renewed, Assigned to Williamson Music and The Estate Of Lorenz Hart
All Rights on behalf of The Estate Of Lorenz Hart Administered by WB Music Corp.
International Copyright Secured   All Rights Reserved

The Wizard of Oz

Music: Harold Arlen
Lyrics: E. Y. Harburg
Screenplay: Noel Langley, Florence Ryerson, Edgar Allan Woolf (John Lee Mahin uncredited)
Produced by: Mervyn LeRoy for MGM
Directed by: Victor Fleming (King Vidor uncredited)
Choreography: Bobby Connolly
Photography: Harold Rosson, Allen Darby (Technicolor)
Cast: Judy Garland, Frank Morgan, Ray Bolger, Bert Lahr, Jack Haley, Billie Burke, Margaret Hamilton, Charley Grapewin, Clara Blandick
Songs: "Over the Rainbow"; "Ding-Dong! The Witch Is Dead"; "We're Off to See the Wizard"; "Follow the Yellow Brick Road"; "If I Only Had a Brain"; "The Merry Old Land of Oz"; "If I Were King of the Forest"
Released: August 1939; 101 minutes

The Tin Woodman (Jack Haley), the Cowardly Lion (Bert Lahr), Dorothy (Judy Garland), and the Scarecrow (Ray Bolger) are met at the Emerald City by the Gate Keeper (Frank Morgan).

The huge success scored by Walt Disney's *Snow White and the Seven Dwarfs* inevitably prompted Hollywood's leading studios to search for other children's fantasies. A logical choice was L. Frank Baum's classic *The Wonderful Wizard of Oz*, written in 1900, which had been adapted as a Broadway musical in 1903 (with the title minus the word "Wonderful"), starring Dave Montgomery and Fred Stone as the Tin Woodman and the Scarecrow. Samuel Goldwyn acquired the screen rights in 1933 and sold them to MGM five years later. Mervyn LeRoy, who had just joined MGM as a producer, and Arthur Freed, who wanted to be a producer, both claimed that he was the one who had persuaded studio boss Louis B. Mayer to make the purchase. Mayer appointed LeRoy as producer and Freed as his assistant.

Three directors, Richard Thorpe, George Cukor, and Lewis Milestone, were assigned before LeRoy settled on Victor Fleming, though the final three weeks of shooting were taken over by King Vidor when Fleming had to report for work on *Gone With the Wind*. (Vidor directed the pivotal "Over the Rainbow" scene, which was almost cut from the film.) The movie made a star of 16-year-old Judy Garland, who played Dorothy, after Mayer was unsuccessful in borrowing Shirley Temple from Fox. Others in the cast were Ray Bolger as the Scarecrow (though the part had originally been given to Buddy Ebsen), Jack Haley as the Tin Woodman (after Ebsen, switched to this part, was hospitalized when the aluminum dust sprayed on his face had gotten into his lungs), Frank Morgan as the Wizard (after the part had been turned down by W. C. Fields and Ed Wynn), and Margaret Hamilton as the Wicked Witch of the West (though LeRoy had initially wanted Gale Sondergaard). Bert Lahr, as the Cowardly Lion, was everyone's choice from the start.

In the screen treatment, Dorothy Gale, unhappy on her drab, sepia-tinted Kansas farm, is knocked out during a tornado (actually a 35-foot windsock made of muslin) and dreams that she is over the rainbow in the colorful land of Oz. There she meets the adorable Munchkins (played by 124 midgets) and goes off on the Yellow Brick Road to see the all-powerful Wizard in the Emerald City. Despite the machinations of the Wicked Witch of the West, Dorothy and her new friends, the Scarecrow, the Tin Woodman, and the Cowardly Lion, complete the journey only to discover that the Wizard is a fraud. He does, however, convince the little girl's companions that they already possess the desired brains, heart, and courage, and Dorothy wakes up from her dream convinced that there's no place like home.

A cartoon variation, *Journey Back to Oz*, was shown in 1974 (though completed in 1962) with well-known actors doing voice-overs, including Miss Garland's daughter, Liza Minnelli, as Dorothy. An urbanized all-black stage version, *The Wiz*, which opened on Broadway in 1975, was brought to the screen three years later with a cast headed by Diana Ross, Michael Jackson, Nipsey Russell, Ted Ross, Richard Pryor, and Lena Horne. In 1985, a Disney production, *Return to Oz*, combined live actors with assorted animated creatures.

MCA ST; CSP ST. MGM/UA VC.

1939